THE SERMON CONSTRUCTION

T. H. SCAMBLER, B.A., Dip. Ed.

PRINCIPAL

COLLEGE OF THE BIBLE

GLEN IRIS

Victoria

Updated and Revised by Barry L. Davis

Copyright©2013 Barry L. Davis

GodSpeed Publishing

Visit Us for More Great Resources at:
www.amazon.com/author/barrydavis
and
www.pastorshelper.com

Table of Contents

INTRODUCTION

Preaching is still the most popular form of public address. In spite of the fact that hosts of people never hear a sermon in their lives, and the Church is widely proclaimed as decadent, dying or dead, it is still true that week by week more people regularly hear sermons, than, any other kind of public utterance. A good sermon is still likely to top the poll when we achieve the performance of taking a referendum of the entire population as to which kind of public address ranks highest in the thought of the people.

To be sure, preaching is terribly criticized, especially by those who never hear it. Quite a few years ago a world-famous socialist, John Spargo, said: "*It is very doubtful, to my mind, whether all the preaching that will be done in America during the next twelve months, let us say, will add as much to the well-being of America as the work of one honest, efficient farmer, or that of a humble school-teacher in some little red schoolhouse.*" What an indictment! Surely we preachers should creep into our shelters and stay there. But Mr. Spargo confessed, concerning preachers: "*Never in the world before was there a class commanding such a vast hearing.*" Now, that's strange. This preaching which is so futile (Mr. Spargo was writing about the futility of preaching) commands the greatest hearing! Probably the late Sylvester Horne was nearer the mark when he said: "*Preaching can never lose its place so long as the mystery and wonder of the human spirit remain. Amid all the changes of thought and phrase the wonder of conversion remains to be the supreme joy and glory of the preacher.*"

There will always be preachers and preaching, because there will always be men who want a new grip on life, who need strength to battle with temptation, and comfort in the day of sorrow, and who feel their need of the presence and power of God.

There are some subjects concerning which profound thinkers discuss very learnedly, which are as clear as day to the initiated, and preaching is one of them. There are men who hear the call of God to enter into the ministry of the Word, there are many who feel a divine urge to preach, and there are hosts (in the aggregate, if not in individual congregations) who listen to preaching as the message of God.

What is the secret of good preaching? A man should not preach at all, unless he has a message. A fondness for talking, a love of display, or a desire for prominence should not be a motive impelling any man to preach. At the back of all really good preaching are a consecrated life, a prepared mind, a gift of utterance and a message to help the souls of men.

What shall we preach? It may be thought that the answer is simple. Preach the Word of God, the message of the Scriptures. That is a good answer, if we understand what it means. It is possible to preach from the Bible and bring no message. We may preach on Bible themes and do nothing but confuse people. A man may use the Bible to promote error. Many people who teach what we consider erroneous doctrines claim to support them with an abundance of Scripture. Men may talk about the contents of the Bible – Bible Geography, Bible History, Natural History, or a host of subjects found in the Bible--chronology, ethnology, genealogy and what not – and never be a preacher. The eighteenth century Deists were experts, many of them, in Bible knowledge, but they were not preachers – they had no message for men's hearts.

The Scriptures present God as a Redeemer and the message of the Book has to do with all that is involved in salvation –

salvation from the guilt, the power, and the consequences of sin. Therefore it is that human need in all its forms – because, all human need is related in some way to the facts of sin and salvation, that becomes the great concern of the preacher. Preaching is the message of the Word of God applied to life; it is that which makes preaching living, vital, and effective. There are preachers who start from the Scriptures, and expound its truth, and apply it to men. There are others who begin with a life situation, and seek the message of the Book relating to it. R.G. Gillie, in "*The Minister and the Modern World,*" spoke of three sources of preaching material: (1) One's own experience; (2) the Bible; and (3) life as we know, it. You may wonder why he did not put the Bible first. His thought was that if we have the right to preach at all, it is because we are witnesses to truth that has been written in our own souls. The fundamental ground of our certainty of sacred truth is what God has done in us. Coleridge once wrote in a letter: "*In the Bible there is more that finds me than I have experienced in all other books put together.*" Thus he believed the Bible was inspired, because it found him at greater depths of his being, and brought with it irresistible evidence of having proceeded from the Holy Spirit. With such an experience as that, a man may well begin to preach to the needs of others, for he is bound to end with the gospel of redemption as revealed in the Bible. From whatever angle we approach this subject, the Word of God is the primal source of the message we have to deliver. Even if a text is not used at the beginning of a sermon, no fault can be found with the message if it is our own, our own witness, which we have received from the Word of God and seek to apply to life.

You wish to preach. We assume then that you have a message. God has spoken to you through his Word. Now you want to become more qualified; to be the best preacher that you can be. James Gibb, in "*Making Proof of the Ministry,*" said that three primary qualifications are a knowledge of God, a knowledge of man and a knowledge of the Bible.

We need to know God in the intimate personal way that grows out of constant communion with Him. It is doubtful if any of us prays enough. Few men really master the discipline of prayer, or gain the knowledge of God that comes alone through "the sweat of the soul." We need to know man in his struggles, his temptations, his sufferings, his sin and his yearning after God. The message, to be effective, should meet these needs of men. That is what makes preaching worthwhile. A preacher may be effective in preaching to an audience of strangers if he deals with the great common needs of human life. But the most effective preacher will be the man who knows the lives of his people – their problems and temptations, their joys and their sorrows, and brings the message of God to meet them. Get to know your Bible.

> *Be diligent to present yourself approved to God, a*
> *worker who does not need to be ashamed, rightly*
> *dividing the word of truth.* – 2 Timothy 2:15

As a preacher you read your Bible for your own devotional life, and that is an essential thing if you are to be a vital preacher. It is part of the process by which you know God. You need to study it also with a view to teaching it. It is possible that a man may find daily nourishment for his spiritual life in the word of God, without his ever coming to a clear understanding of the Scriptures such as a teacher should have. Some people adopt a special diet of scriptural nourishment, and find that it answers their needs very well, but the limited diet they use may be very unsatisfying to people with robust spiritual appetites. A man who aims to preach should know something of the accepted principles of interpretation of the Scriptures. He needs to know the difference between the Old and New Testaments. He should know the main sections of the New Testament, and the purpose of each. Certainly he should know how to direct sinners in the gospel way, and teach disciples the great practical doctrines of the Christian life.

1. The Nature of the Sermon

What is a sermon? The well-known definition of Phelps, in his *The Theory of Preaching,* is useful: "*A sermon is an oral address to the popular mind upon religious truth as contained in the Scriptures, and elaborately treated with a view to persuasion.*" Each phrase is important. Perhaps the most important are the references to the Scriptures and to persuasion. The address will not be a sermon unless it deals with Scriptural truth, and it should have a purpose affecting the hearts and lives of the hearers. In many churches it was common to devote the morning sermon to teaching Christian people, and the evening sermon, to preaching the gospel to the unsaved. In each case it had a Scriptural basis, and was done "with a view to persuasion."

There will be times when the purpose is more in the way of instruction than of persuasion, but the ultimate purpose is always persuasion. It is a mistake to avoid the persuasive note in sermons to Christian people, as though they did not need it since they had accepted the gospel. The apostle Paul said the gospel is the power of God "*to us who are being saved*" (1 Cor. 1:18). The Christian still has great decisions to make, and heights to attain and an exhortation to Christian people may well close with an earnest persuasive note leading to "great resolves of heart" (Judges 5:15).

Vital Preaching

Preaching is vital only when it is directed to people's need. The need may be either unrealized or felt. The preacher will seek to declare the whole counsel of God (Acts 20:27), whether his hearers realize their need of it or not. Such subjects as God, the Savior, the Holy Spirit, Sin, Salvation, Prayer, Christian

Duties, and the Christian Life, constitute a system of truth which every preacher will desire to bring to his congregation. If you want to be a helpful preacher you will give particular attention to the needs of your audience. Dr. Jowett said that when he was preparing a sermon he would bring before his mind a number of people who he knew would be in his congregation--a doctor, a business man, a servant girl, a mother, a clerk – and keep them in view while he constructed his sermon. The idea was not to preach at them (you must never do that), but to preach to them in such a way as to meet their special problems. Try it out. Focus on your audience in the day of preparation. Ask yourself *"Who will be there? How can I help them?"* Don't preach to the absent. Don't preach to yourself, in the sense that you merely follow some line of study in which you are interested, and which you inflict without concern of your audience. If you are observant at all you will know of tempted people, of worried, tired, sad people, to whom you may bring a message of hope.

Preaching at its best is the message of God's Word, brought into contact with human need. Yet this must be done with delicacy and good taste. The indirect line of approach is generally better than the direct. You should not preach to a person's need so directly that he is embarrassed, because he knows, and knows that everybody else knows, that it is intended for him. When you wish to condemn wrong, never let it be by a personal attack upon individuals in the audience. The pulpit is a sheltered and sacred place-it must not be violated to administer personal rebuke. Such work is better done in a personal way, face to face. Until we can do such a duty personally, we are not qualified to do it at all. Even then, it might better be done by the indirect method. Do you remember how the prophet Nathan told King David he was a murderer (2 Sam.12:1-6)? A direct attack might easily have cost the prophet his head; by the indirect approach David was brought to repentance. If you knew there would be people in the congregation with a spirit of resentment towards one another, it probably would not be wise to preach on the subject, *The Sin of Resentment*. Such a subject would certainly help other people to enjoy the sermon – people like sermons that are manifestly directed at the sins of others. It would not, however, kill the spirit of resentment. It would be better to preach a sermon on the forgiving love of Christ (Luke 23:34).

Essential Qualities

Preach with confidence and conviction. The Bible is accepted by your hearers as the Word of God. You do not need to argue about it. There is little need to prove the Bible is inspired. People who come to church already believe it. Proclaim *"O earth, earth, earth, Hear the word of the LORD!"* (Jer. 22:29).

Preach with sympathy. To be of service, a preacher must love people, all kinds of people, with their virtues, and vices, their greatness and their pettiness, their sorrows and their struggles. He will be a man of understanding and patience, not critical of people's weakness, or overbearing towards their faults.

Preach with sincerity. Men yearn for reality today perhaps more than anything else. They hate sham and pretense. Do not try to preach if you are not genuine and sincere and true. It you are not, you cannot hide the fact for long. You may not have the gifts that make a great orator. You may never be eloquent. Few are. Yet you may have those qualities which will make men want to hear you. People like to listen to a man who is genuinely true and sincere. The personal factor in preaching is of primary importance. Do not be a mere wire, carrying a message, nor a talking machine. The only perfect expression in preaching is through a preacher's own heart and life. It is the large infusion of personal force that made men flock to hear H. Emerson Fosdick, E. Stanley Jones, J. Fort Newton, and other well-known preachers. We may never be great preachers, but we may have that essential quality – sincerity. Kennard wrote: *"The preacher's soul is a prism through which the white and dazzling light of spiritual truth passes, and, receives in its passing human coloring and refraction along the lines of human want and sensibility."* If you aspire to share in the ministry of preaching in the Church, yield yourself to God in full consecration. Strive with eager care that you may be worthy before God, to whom all hearts are open, and all desires known – that will be your best commendation to the people to whom you preach. After you have acquired the art of sermon building, there will be other things to learn if you are to be a good preacher For instance, you must make your sermon interesting. The outline of the sermon, which we are to study, definitely will help in that direction. But more than that will be necessary. A sermon may be technically correct in its construction, but deadly dull in its delivery, or in its development of thought. Someone has said, *"There are preachers whom you cannot listen to, there are preachers whom you can listen to, and there are preachers whom you must listen to."* J. Paterson Smyth used to tell his students, *"You CAN make people listen."* Many elements enter into it – clearness, directness, illustration, diction, and the will to succeed. A great English preacher said: *"Whenever I address men I determine that they shall listen."* And they did. Let us keep these things in mind as we address ourselves to our special task of sermon building.

2. First Steps in Sermon Construction

The preparation of a sermon is partly conditioned by the demands for our services. Our names are on a circuit plan, or we have a regular appointment, or we are ministers in charge of churches, and we must preach according to arrangement. We cannot wait until we are given a definite message, or until we are moved by the Spirit of God. The prophets presumably did that – they spoke only when they heard the voice of God, and their messages live until this day. But we must speak whenever necessity or convention demands it. Even so, it should always be true that we have a message. By virtue of our ability to preach at all, we are in a sense shepherds of the flock. We ought therefore to have their needs on our hearts. There are subjects on which they need instruction. Let us remember that we are not asked to preach for our own sakes, but for the sake of others. We select our sermon topics in view of these facts.

Sometimes the nature of our message is determined by special seasons, as Christmas and Easter, or recognized festivals, like anniversaries or harvest festivals. Churches which observe the Church Year are accustomed to hear sermons on the appropriate lessons from the Gospels or the Epistles suitable to the various seasons of the year. Whatever the day or the occasion, let us realize that we stand as the messengers of God, commissioned by Him to speak His Word.

Value of Outline

You have chosen your subject – what then? How may you best present it to the congregation? It is well to have an outline, to keep your thoughts in order. It is a pity when a sermon lacks coherence or plan. Good ideas may be lost by the hearer, interesting illustrations may fail to admit the light, and choice language may seem pointless, all because the sermon followed no principle of construction. A good outline gives order and sequence to the thoughts presented. The outline of the sermon is what the bony framework is to the body. A skeleton is not of much value by itself, but when it is covered by living tissue it is of tremendous importance.

A sermon outline does two things at least:

1. It is of great help to the preacher in thinking through his subject.

2. It helps the people to understand and remember the message.

I recently heard a doctor addressing a Christian assembly. He said he had never preached a sermon in his life, and did not go much on first point, second point, etc... But before he was through his address he said. *"There was a third thing I wanted to say,"* and he betrayed the fact that he was following good homiletical procedure after all, and we remembered what he said all the better because he was using a mental outline and had three lessons he was emphasizing. You may find that good ideas are hazy in your own mind until you sort them out in some outline form. It is very important in preaching that the preacher be clear in his own grasp of ideas, and in the expression of them. You will never make them clear to other people if they are not clear to you. The arrangement of our thoughts in an outline is one of the best means of accomplishing that end.

An outline not only helps the preacher to clarify his thought; it helps him to develop thinking. It is a creative process. Dr. Johnson, according to Boswell, said: *"The divisions not only help the memory of the hearer, but direct the judgment of the writer; they supply sources of invention, and keep every part in its proper place."*

Note that statement: They supply sources of invention. Many preachers without a large background of material are often puzzled about how to go to work to find it. Anything that will supply sources of invention is important, and that is one of the functions of the outline.

Question the Text

You have been attracted by a text. You sense its value and truth. But how can you amplify its statement, illustrate its truth, and discover enough material to occupy the time for an address? One of the first lessons I ever learned was to question the text. Ask: "*Who? What? Why? Where? When? How?*" Take, for instance, a text like Romans 4:3b:

> *For what does the Scripture say?* "ABRAHAM BELIEVED GOD, AND IT WAS ACCOUNTED TO HIM FOR RIGHTEOUSNESS."

To answer those questions about this text you will be obliged to go both to the context in Romans 4, and to the story of Abraham in Genesis. When you have read those passages carefully and thoughtfully, and have answered the questions, you will have quite a lot of information concerning a man's history, and an important doctrine. You will have quite enough material for a sermon as long as you ought to try to preach at this stage. You will also have the basis of an outline. You could take three or four of the most suggestive of these questions, and make them your main headings. You might even leave them in question form, and make your answer to each the material for the sermon, thus:

1. What was Paul trying to prove?
2. How did Abraham show he believed God?
3. Why was it reckoned to him for righteousness?

4. How does this prove Paul's point?

Later we will talk about introductions and conclusions and subdivisions, but at present we are concerned in getting at the chief ideas which provide the main headings of the sermon.

Dr. James Black, in *The Mystery of Preaching*, emphasizes the same idea. "*When I have my text or subject, I put a series of questions to it, and try to answer them. I box its ears something like this: What do you mean? What did you mean for that man in his own day? Why was he led to say this? ... And are you true always? Do you mean the same for me today? What would it mean for me if I accepted what you teach? What principles or duties do you involve for me? ... What must I do to make your message real and true in my own life? How can I illustrate modernly what you teach for myself and others?*" You will notice that Dr. Black's questions ask for the meaning of the words when they were written, and the truth of them, but particularly concerning their meaning and truth for us today. That is how a great preacher applies Scripture teaching to life. We must all learn to do that, more or less. It would repay you richly as a preacher if you memorized those questions from Dr. Black, as you would learn a poem. If you can ask questions of a text in that way, and can answer them at all intelligently, you could hardly fail to be an interesting preacher. It means work, of course – hard work. To be a worthwhile preacher you must be prepared to work.

Plan No. 1

Let us call this questioning idea Plan No. 1.

It has been my experience that students require time to appreciate the value of this question method, and to use it to advantage. Sometimes there is a lack of imagination, but there is often a suspicion that there has been a lack of sufficiently hard work. Cultivate the habit of asking many questions, so that when you have answered them you have sufficient material for a sermon.

Let us take another example – Hebrews 11:24-26:

> *By faith Moses, when he became of age, refused to be called the son of Pharaoh's daughter, choosing rather to suffer affliction with the people of God than to enjoy the passing pleasures of sin, esteeming the reproach of Christ greater riches than the treasures in Egypt; for he looked to the reward.*

Now for your questions. It would pay you to pause here and ask your own questions and compare them with what follows.

What are the historical facts behind this text? (You must read Exodus to get them.) What were the circumstances when Moses became of age that made a choice necessary? What choices did he make? What afflictions did he suffer because of his choice? What does the reproach of Christ mean? What did he renounce? What was involved in being the son of Pharaoh's daughter? What pleasures of sin were meant in Moses' case? Is sin pleasurable? What treasures of Egypt would have been his had he done the other thing? What enabled him to make such a great renunciation and such a choice? What is faith? How does it act to make such choices possible? Is my faith strong enough to make me do something worthwhile? Will my faith stand in a crisis? Is there any great renunciation I should make? Are there any great choices, fraught with big consequences, that I should make?

You see there are many questions you may ask a text. Some of them, and the answers, may be useless for your purpose. But out of them all, when by diligence and hard work, you have answered them; you will have abundance of material for a sermon. We have not studied introductions and conclusions yet, but you would not find it difficult to provide them here. Your answers may suggest an outline like this:

Introduction.--Briefly tell the story of Moses, leading up to this crisis in his life.

I.   **Great Faith**
        A. What faith is.
        B. How faith works.
II.   **Great Renunciation.**
        A. Position and honor.
        B. The pleasures of sin.
        C. The treasures of Egypt.
III.   **Great Choices.**
        A. Choosing affliction.
        B. Accepting the reproach of Christ.

For a conclusion, apply the lesson to our own lives, testing our faith, our choices, and the renunciation we must make.

If you did not attempt what was earlier suggested, and do your own reading in Exodus and study the text for yourself, and ask your own questions, and answer them, the above outline will be just an outline. But if you really worked at it, you have a stock of interesting material good enough for any congregation, which if presented in this form with earnestness and power, would bring a living message to human hearts.

For Review:

1. Discuss the values of an outline in (a) the preparation and (b) the delivery of a sermon.

2. What is the essential value of the question method outlined in this chapter?

3. Prepare outlines of sermons on Hebrews 11:4 and James 5:16b-17 using Plan No. 1.

3. Sermon Building

Sometimes a text will disclose its beauty to you if you simply underline its phrases, or clauses, or even its most important words, one by one, and use them as the leading ideas in the outline. Take, for instance, Matthew 13:44:

> *"Again, the kingdom of heaven is like treasure hidden in a field, which a man found and hid; and for joy over it he goes and sells all that he has and buys that field."*

That simple bit of underlining gives you the following interesting result:

1. The Kingdom of Heaven

2. Is a Treasure

3. Which is Hidden, but

4. May be Found, and when it is found

5. A Man will Give all he has to Possess it.

Now that statement, in five parts, itself constitutes the main headings of a first-class sermon outline. Or it may be re-arranged. Make the subject "The Kingdom of Heaven," and the outline thus

I. Its Value: A Treasure

II. Its Concealed Value: Hidden in a Field

III. Its Discovered Value: When it is Found

IV. Its Absolute Worth: "sells all that he has and buys."

That is merely an outline, but it asserts some profound truths that any man who has had experience of God could enlarge upon. You will not therefore find it difficult to develop the subject. You may know there is a great deal of discussion as to what exactly the kingdom is. You do not at present need to enter into that, nor be restrained by it. It is safe to say that no

one knows all that our Lord had in mind by his various uses of the word *Kingdom*. But it is also safe to say that the word is applied to all the various aspects of man's submission to God's sovereignty – it is always God's reign in the hearts of men. It is safe to say that here the Teacher was thinking of the gospel, and all that it is to man. Keep the idea of the gospel in your mind, and begin your development of the text. It will help you still if you use the question method. How is the gospel a treasure? All the message of redemption and hope can be discussed there. Why is the value of the gospel hidden to men? Why is it not appreciated? You could say some useful things about that. How may a man find the value of the gospel? The answer to that is within the range of your Christian experience. And will a man surrender everything in the world for Christ and his gospel? Yes, and you can tell why, if you are called to preach. When you have done a little work along that line you have an outline and material sufficient for an instructive sermon.

Take now another text, Hebrews 2:3a, and underline it:

How shall we escape if we neglect so great a salvation?

At once you have a simple and effective outline.

> I. A Pertinent Question: "How shall we escape?"
>
> II. The Peril of Neglect: "If we neglect."
>
> III. A Great Salvation: "So great a salvation."

With practice you will soon learn to develop ingenuity in handling a text. This one, for instance, might be more effective if you dealt with the main points in the reverse order to that in which they are found in the text. The subject of the text, in a sense, is the great salvation; that naturally comes first. The pertinent question is a sort of application; that would better come last. So your arrangement will be:

I. A Great Salvation.
II. The Peril of Neglect.
III. A Pertinent Question.

You will always feel free to expound a text in any order that will discover its meaning and apply its lessons.

We still have only the main outlines. How shall we find the material to talk about? Well, you use your knowledge, and you exercise your imagination, and you go to work. You must work.

Application to Task

For years I had on my desk a stimulating bit of advice for a man who is about to prepare a sermon. It was this: *"Get a piece of cobbler's wax, put in on your chair, and sit on it."* It needs application to the task.

Take then the first point, *A Great Salvation.* You may ask Salvation from what? Answers immediately spring to your mind: Salvation from the guilt of sin, from the power of sin, from a life of ineffectiveness, from the fear and dread of the tomb. Take the other word in the first main division: Great! How is this salvation great? Albert Barnes' commentary, written many years ago, but still of very great value to anyone who is learning to preach, answers the question in this way

This salvation is great

1. Because its author is great;

2. Because it saves from great sins

3. Because it saves from great dangers;

4. Because it is effective by infinite displays of power, wisdom and love.

We are now developing sub-divisions, under our main divisions, and soon we shall need to discuss these sub-divisions. In the meantime we shall note that here is a way to make the sermon grow. When you have a little material on each of these points, and perhaps have given an illustration or two, it will be time to move on to the next main division, because the people will soon be wanting to go home to dinner.

The Peril of Neglect! What are the perils of neglect in any department of life, in education, in gardening, in business? You can tell, and you could apply the lesson. Set your ideas out in so many definite points, so that you can discuss them one by one.

A Pertinent Question! A preacher once said that he was about to ask a question which he could not answer, and which his hearers could not answer, which angels could not answer, nor the devil, nor even God himself. How shall we escape if we neglect so great a salvation?

I have illustrated at some length this method of outlining a text in order to discover the leading ideas for the main divisions of the sermon. All texts may not be dealt with so readily, but we shall come to other means of dealing with them presently.

Plan No. 2

Let us call this outlining method Plan No. 2.

Another useful method is to take an important word, like faith or grace, or the name of a person, and with the use of a concordance select a number of texts dealing with the subject. Then build up your sermon from the thoughts suggested by the text. Take, for example, the word SIN. Here are some texts,

all chosen because they are in a sense definitions of sin.

1. Proverbs 24:9 – Devising foolishness is sin.

2. James 4:17 – The person who knows to do good and does not do *IT,* to him it is sin.

3. Romans 14:23 – Whatever is not of faith is sin.

4. 1 John 3:4 – Whoever commits sin, commits lawlessness.

5. 1 John 5:17 – All unrighteousness is sin.

With five such clear statements as to what sin is, we are able to find a satisfactory outline covering a wide range of discussion on the subject. We may give it the title *The Meaning of Sin*, and adopt the following main divisions for the sermon:

I. The Evil Thought.
II. The Neglect of Duty.
III. Ignoring One's Conscience.
IV. Disobedience to God's Law.
V. Doing Wrong to Others.

I need hardly take time here to develop those points. The earlier examples will show how it is done.

Look now at the following texts: John 6:35; John 8:12; John 10:11; John 11:25. You will have noticed that each one contains one of the great assertions of Jesus beginning with "I AM." That is the connecting link between these passages. It will not be a difficult matter to build up an outline, using titles suggested by each text in turn. Let me merely suggest a title for the sermon as a whole – *The Sufficiency of Christ*.

In this chapter we have been dealing chiefly with outlines. Much of the work of development is yet to be done. Not all,

however, for when you have achieved a good outline you have already produced much of the material of which the sermon will consist.

For Review:

1. For the outline on Hebrews 2:3a, find points for discussion of the Main Division II., The Peril of Neglect.

2. Write Romans 1:16, underline it as suggested in Plan No. 2, and construct main divisions of an outline, with titles. (That is, do not merely write down the different sentences.)

3. Construct an outline (main divisions only) on *The Conditions of Prevailing Prayer*. For this, use a concordance and a reference Bible to discover the most helpful texts.

4. The Structure of a Sermon

We have been studying the value of an outline, and we should now be ready to study it in its complete form. Phelps' book analyses a sermon as follows: The Text, Explanation, Introduction, Proposition, Division, Development, and Conclusion. Now, that seems very elaborate and formal, and it is. It is too cumbersome for us these modern days. But each part has value, and we shall be able to prepare sermons all the better if we have at the back of our minds a knowledge of the complete process. After the text which we have already considered we

Explanation

An explanation may or may not be necessary. If the words of your text are clear in meaning, no opening explanation is required. If a text is obscure in its terms, or if it has historical or biographical allusions, or is expressed in metaphor, it may be advantageous, even necessary, to make an explanation at the beginning. I have a harvest thanksgiving sermon in Isaiah 28:23-29: *"For the black cummin is not threshed with a threshing sledge, Nor is a cartwheel rolled over the cummin; But the black cummin is beaten out with a stick, And the cummin with a rod. Bread* FLOUR *must be ground, etc.,"* I call it *A Parable in Agriculture*, but I feel that an explanation is necessary before I begin to preach its message.

Introduction

The introduction includes anything that is done to secure a natural approach to the subject. In this sense an explanation may be an introduction. It may, however, be necessary at times to prepare a congregation for the discussion you intend to present. You may need to draw interest at the beginning in a subject that has no appeal in itself. You may need to awaken sympathy with your line of approach. An introduction to a sermon is similar to getting a point of contact with a Sunday school class for a lesson. Preachers do not always give as much attention to it as teachers are taught to do.

I asked my class – beginners in the art of sermon construction – to present an introduction to the sermon, *The Meaning of Sin*, which we outlined previously (Chapter 3). Here is one that was submitted:

1. Sin is a reality and has existed since the time of Adam.

2. Sin has persisted throughout the world's history and has been punished by God – Noah.

3. Sin has caused the downfall of nation after nation. Give examples of this.

4. Sin in the world today is a real thing.

5. What then is the meaning of sin?

It was not by any means the best introduction submitted, nor necessarily the poorest. It bears the marks of inexperience, which often tends to sweep over all history in an introduction. It lacks definiteness. It certainly lacks interest. A congregation might easily go to sleep under an introduction like that, unless it became interested, as it often does, in the personality of a young preacher for his own sake. One of the introductions submitted was an interesting and pertinent illustration; it was a good introduction. Another was a striking quotation from one of Whittier's poems, also very suitable, and it achieved its purpose. Most of the others were similar in conception and execution to the one quoted above – too general, indefinite and heavy to be good introductions. There may come a time when the nature of the subject or the occasion may require a lengthy and ponderous introduction. It will not often come. Hear, O Israel! The introduction to a sermon must be concise, definite and interesting.

Here are some general principles, then, governing the use of introductions. Recognize their importance, make them brief, and be sure they are well thought out. Your sermon may be made or marred by the introduction. Generally it should be prepared last, just as you would build a house first and the porch afterwards.

The material of the introduction may be anything that will serve to introduce the subject to the congregation. It may, as we saw, be an explanation of the text; it may, if the text is taken from a narrative, be the story of which it is a part; it may be information about the author of the book from which the text is taken; it may be a description of the book itself. The reasons which led you to select the subject may make a good introduction, or it may be a suitable illustration. Do not let it be an apology.

Proposition

The word that is used for proposition in more modern works is "Theme." It is simply a definite statement of the subject to be discussed. Sometimes the text expresses the theme. If your text is *"It is a faithful saying, and worthy of all acceptation, that Christ Jesus came into the world to save sinners,"* the statement is definite enough to constitute the theme, and no other is needed. Were you preaching on the text we studied in Chapter 3 on Matthew 13:44 concerning the kingdom of heaven, it would be a good thing to define your purpose in the sermon: *"The gospel is of such value that it is worth the surrender of all we have to possess it."*

A text may sometimes express more than the subject you intend to discuss and a title may be too limited, and for the sake of clarity you need to express in a proposition the specific subject you intend to work out in the sermon. There must be a clear, definite purpose in your own mind, if your sermon is to have the quality of grip. Dr. J. H. Jowett said that if an angel halted a preacher when he was entering the pulpit and asked him for his message he should be able to state it in one clear crystal sentence. If you have such a clear sentence, and present it to your hearers, that becomes the expression of your theme.

Young preachers, in stating their themes, tend to become wordy and weighty, and therefore become guilty of the same fault we have criticized in the introductions. Think your subject through, and state your theme in crisp, clear definite words, avoiding as far as possible subordinate and qualifying clauses.

Frequently the proposition or theme is not a formal part of the sermon, but it should be in the preacher's mind. It will sometimes happen that it is better not to state the purpose at the beginning. Interest may be maintained by holding the minds of the people in suspense.

Where you have a vast subject, such as God, Immortality, etc., you must necessarily narrow your subject down to some definite point of view. Under Immortality, for instance, you may discuss the proof of immortality, or the power of immortality, and that particular definition becomes your theme.

Division and Development

Division refers to the principal sections into which the main part of the sermon is divided, and has been discussed in part already, and will be dealt with more fully later. Already, also, you have some definite ideas about the process of development – of amplifying, unfolding and enlarging upon the outline you have prepared. The outline is the skeleton; the development is the flesh which covers the bones. It is a creative process, and is often most difficult for the beginner. Granted a little knowledge (your aspiration to preach suggests that you have something in your mind and heart you long to tell), and a little imagination (you will never be a preacher without something of that quality of mind) and a willingness to work – WORK – and you will learn the secret. There are ways of doing it – definite lines to follow. Plan No. 1 (Chapter 2), for constructing outlines, is indispensable in developing your material too. Ask your subject questions – every aspect of it, especially what it means and how it applies to life today.

Another thing you may do is to take a sheet of paper and a pencil, and sit down to think and write. Put your subject at the head of the sheet, and put down everything that suggests itself to your mind that has relation to it. Do not worry about the order, or an outline at this stage. Think, and write, and continue to apply your mind diligently to the task in hand. I am trying to suggest to you a very strenuous process. You will not, in the middle of this operation, attend to a neglected telephone call, or read e-mail while you wait for thoughts to come. Earlier I spoke of sweat of soul; now I am thinking of sweat of mind. That may be a real experience. It is much easier to chop wood than to think your way through the development of a sermon. For a grim half an hour, an hour, you hold yourself to the task, concentrating, writing down ideas, illustrations, passages of scripture or other quotations, until you have a mass of uncoordinated material that will be useful the next day or the day after when you come to the subject again. It should be left for another day too, after this process of intense application is finished. You will not try to form this undeveloped mass into an outline – not yet. When you come back to the subject later your mind will be fresh, but more than that, you will find that your unconscious mind has been at work, apparently without effort, on the material you had written out, and has prepared the way for a moderately easy passage to the completed sermon.

Conclusion

This is the work of bringing your sermon to such an end as will satisfy the minds of your hearers and perhaps bring their hearts to decision.

The conclusion is important; perhaps the most important part of the sermon. This is where you clinch your argument; this is where you determine your results. To fail here is to fail altogether. Yet it is often neglected, and left to take care of itself. Prepare your conclusion.

The conclusion may be a summary of the discourse. This is a useful thing to do, to reiterate the main parts of the sermon so that they may be impressed on the hearer's mind. Generally it should be more than that. There should be an application. You are working for results; end on the personal note. A very effective conclusion may be helped by a well-conceived illustration. In gospel sermons, we have an excellent opportunity of concluding in a direct and personal way. Even when we are exhorting Christian people we should, as a rule, conclude in a manner that will leave an emotional sense in the soul of the people which will contribute to the high attainments to which we are calling them.

A few pointed practical questions may make a good conclusion. You have been preaching about the Savior. "*What will you do with Jesus? Is your heart ready to respond to His call?*

Has He opened the way for you to reach your highest achievements of character? Can you reach your highest ideals without Him? Will you yield your life to the control of the Master of men?"

Quite often a simple pertinent heartfelt prayer is a good conclusion. Or it may be that a suitable word of Scripture will provide the conclusion you need. *"He who has an ear, let him hear what the Spirit says to the churches."*

Reviewing these factors in the make-up of a sermon you will notice that the first three things (or four, if we include the text) are all introductory, and the next two belong to the body of the sermon. Therefore, we may say that a sermon consists of three parts: Introduction, development and conclusion. You will not, in your work, be likely to be very elaborate in the formal set-out of your sermons. Probably we all tend to become a little indifferent to form after a while. There is a great difference, however, between an inattention to forms that has a disciplined technique behind it, and one that springs from ignorance. At this stage you must be subject to forms, if some day you wish to be a master who can safely ignore them.

For Review:

1. Find a suitable theme for the sermon on *Moses* outlined at the end of Chapter 2.

2. Suggest a suitable introduction and conclusion to the sermon on *The Meaning of Sin* at the end of Chapter 3.

5. Structure of a Sermon (Continued)

Preaching is an intensely personal art. Every man with a soul on fire, and a message to deliver, will have his own way of presenting the truth. Preaching should be the enthusiastic and joyous utterance of a living experience. To the extent that it is so it is difficult to confine it within rules.

Technique

Like every other art, however, preaching has a technique, the knowledge of which helps to clarify expression and correct faults of workmanship. The musician studies the rules of expression and harmony; the painter studies the mechanism of his art – the composition of paints, the making of brushes and the forms he is to portray. So, too, does the preacher need to study the art of sermon construction, the psychology of an audience and the principles of delivery.

We have emphasized the value of an outline, and have studied the place and value of the theme. We are now going to study more definitely the construction of sermon divisions.

An outline consists of main divisions, subdivisions, and perhaps further divisions which we may identify as sub-subdivisions. Study the following example carefully. Introduction and conclusion are omitted.

CONVERSION OF A PREACHER
Acts 18:24-28

I. THE PREACHER. Apollos.
    A. A Jew. (24).

B. Foreign born. (24).

C. Eloquent. (24).

D. Mighty in the Scriptures. (24). This involves:
    (a) Knowledge of the Scriptures.
    (b) Moral and spiritual qualities, such as conviction.

E. Was instructed in the way of the Lord. (25).
    (a) He taught concerning Jesus. (25).
    (b) Yet his knowledge was deficient. (25).

F. Fervent in spirit. (29).

G. He had the courage of his convictions. (26)

II. PERSONAL WORKERS. Priscilla and Aquila. They were

A. Jews (Acts 18:2), who were banished from Rome.

B. Co-workers with Paul. (Rom. 16:3).
    (a) As tentmakers (Acts 18:3).
    (b) As Christian workers. Church met in their house. (Rom. 16:5).
    (c) They had risked lives for Paul. (Rom. 16:4).

III. CONVERSION OF APOLLOS.

A. Due to Priscilla and Aquila. (26).
    (a) They saw his deficiency.
    (b) They sought opportunity to help him. "they took him aside."
    (c) They instructed him.

B. Apollos was teachable.
    (a) He accepted the instruction.
    (b) Afterwards he had a new message.

You will realize, afresh, the value of an outline. When you have sorted out the ideas in this passage of Scripture, and related passages, you will see the force of the statement in Chapter 2 that divisions supply sources of invention. When you have made yourself familiar with the details as outlined, you will see that you could enlarge a little on each point, and even if it were only a sentence or two, you would have the material for a substantial address.

I suggest that you memorize this outline, so that you have fixed indelibly in your mind the form of a good outline. (I usually learn my outlines by heart, and when I am preaching I do not need to make much use of notes. The more attention you give to notes, the less you have for your audience, and the less interesting your message becomes.)

You will notice that in the outline there are three main divisions. They are indicated by Roman numerals, and written in capitals. Main divisions do not need to be limited to just three. One of the jokes made in the presence of preachers is about the "three points and a poem" of a sermon. They are always made, of course, by people who do not know anything about homiletics, and who apparently never listen very carefully to sermons. Main divisions may be only two, or they may be four or five, as the subject requires. It is wise not to have too many, for the sake of people's memories. Perhaps the reason why some people think that sermons always have three main divisions is that this is the kind most easily remembered.

Main Divisions

Now note a very important thing about these main divisions – they cover the whole of the material. There is nothing in the sub-divisions, etc., which is not included in the main divisions. All the facts about Apollos that are mentioned in the sub-divisions rightly come under the main division: "I. THE PREACHER." A primary rule about main divisions, then, is that they should include or cover all the text, or all the subject to be discussed.

Another rule is, the main divisions should not contain what is not included in the text or subject. To illustrate, in chapter 19:1-6 is the story of twelve men who knew the baptism of

John, but lacked complete knowledge of the gospel. Paul instructed them, and re-baptized them. Their case was in some respects similar to that of Apollos. But we are not told that Apollos was re-baptized. Was he? That is an interesting question. You might like to discuss it a little in your sermon. Only a little though! You must not let a speculative subject like that crowd out the essential parts of the sermon. If you did include it in your sermon, it could not be made a main division, because it is not really included in the subject; it is just an interesting question that comes up incidentally, because the two narratives are consecutive, and concern the same sort of people. Its proper place would really be in the sub-sub-divisions, under III.B., and between (a) and (b).

Another rule is, avoid using subordinate ideas in the text or subject as main headings. For instance, in the sermon outlined, the seven sub-divisions dealing with Apollos are all subordinate, and are included under the main heading, "I. THE PREACHER." It would not be good construction work to use one of these sub-divisions, such as No. 4 (D.), "Mighty in the Scriptures," important though it is, as a main division.

Finally, keep your main divisions unified in design. In this outline they are all titles, as follows

I. The Preacher;
II. Personal Workers;
III. Conversion of Apollos.

They could have been expressed as:

I. The Preacher;
II. Priscilla and Aquila were good personal workers;
III. How was Apollos brought into fuller light?

But that is clumsy. One is a title, the second a statement, and the third a question. As far as possible make them all alike – all titles, or all statements, or all questions. It is quite a good thing sometimes to use the statement or propositional form, or the question form, if the one form is used throughout.

Perhaps even more important than the main divisions of the sermon are the sub-divisions. The main divisions indicate the general order of the discussion, but the sub-divisions deal with the subject matter directly.

The main divisions are the picture frame; the sub-divisions are the picture itself. When you have sketched out the main divisions you have only begun the work of preparation; the essential work of preparation is yet to be done. Sub-divisions are the parts into which the main divisions naturally divide themselves. Look again at our outline. Even though you have learned it, it will help you to see the setup again. Very naturally the sub-divisions of the first main division, The Preacher, will consist of the facts that are recorded about the preacher. You will see that while the main headings are important as covering the range of study to be followed in the sermon, the substance of the sermon is in the sub-divisions. The same thing is true of the sub-sub-divisions, when the separate points of the subdivisions need to be indicated. There are a number of things that a clear working out of the subdivisions will do for you:

1. It will help you to readily recall the parts of your sermon;

2. It will help you to avoid repetition;

3. It will protect you against long-windedness;

4. It will help you to preserve the unity of your sermon.

Sub-divisions

Where shall we find our sub-divisions? This is important, for it is where the secret of successful development of the sermon material lies. There are various sources of sub-divisions. In the outline we are studying you will see that all the sub-divisions under Main Division I. are from the passage of scripture used as a text (Acts 18:24-28). The same thing is true of Main Division III. But the sub-divisions under Main Division II. are from other passage of Scripture which deal with these personal workers. You may also notice that the sub-sub-divisions (a) and (b) under I, D., are not really stated in the Scripture at all, but are matters that are implied in or inferred from the text. Here, then, in this one outline are indicated at least three sources of sub-divisions. In the next chapter we shall study them more fully.

One other thing you should notice about our outline – the way the different divisions are indicated on the page.

The main divisions are in capitals and are numbered with Roman numerals, and they all begin the same distance from the margin.

The sub-divisions are numbered with capital letters and all begin at the same distance from the margin, too, but further in than the main headings.

The sub-sub-divisions are further in again, and are numbered with lower case letters in parentheses.

You may, of course, use your own method, but make it uniform, so that you know at a glance just what part you are dealing with. Such a system will also greatly help your memory – it is easy to get a clear visual picture of the outline.

For Review:

1. Reproduce the outline of the sermon "Conversion of a Preacher."

2. State the rules governing the use of main headings.

3. Discuss the importance of sub-divisions.

4. What sources of sub-divisions have been indicated?

6. Sources of Sub-Divisions

In our study of the sermon outline, "Conversion of a Preacher" (Chapter 5), we saw that there were three kinds of sub-divisions used:

1. Those gathered from the text itself;

2. Those culled from other passages;

3. Those that were implied in or inferred from the text.

The use of sub-divisions (and also the finer points, which we have called sub-sub-divisions) is so important in sermon construction, that it will be well to investigate their sources a little more fully. We shall begin with those we have already used.

1. Sub-divisions may be supplied by the text itself. Some texts are particularly rich in this way. See Paul's statement in 2 Timothy 4:7-8:

> I have fought the good fight, I have finished the race, I have kept the faith. Finally, there is laid up for me the crown of righteousness, which the Lord, the righteous Judge, will give to me on that Day, and not to me only but also to all who have loved His appearing.

You will see that the text naturally takes two main divisions, which cover the whole passage:

I. PAUL'S BACKWARD GLANCE, "I have fought ... kept the faith."

II. PAUL'S FORWARD LOOK, "Finally ... His appearing."

The text itself provides excellent sub-divisions. They are:

I. PAUL'S BACKWARD GLANCE (v. 7).

A. The good soldier: "I have fought the good fight."

B. The strenuous runner: "I have finished the race."

C. The faithful disciple: "I have kept the faith."

II. PAUL'S FORWARD LOOK (v. 8).

A. The victor's crown: "Finally…the crown of righteousness."

B. The day of triumph: "Which the Lord ... on that Day."

C. The general hope: "and not to me only ... His appearing."

Every text is not so rich in suggestive outlines as this one. Many may not provide the sub-divisions at all, and other sources become necessary. The first thing, however, is to examine the text to see if it will provide any or all the required sub-divisions.

One curious thing we may note here. While the two verses we are considering are well covered by two main divisions, if we selected the seventh verse alone for our text, we should naturally have three main divisions – the shorter text would require more main divisions than the longer one. The reason why is clear at a glance. "I have fought the good fight, I have finished the race, I have kept the faith."

What were the sub-divisions for the larger text now become the main divisions for the smaller text. You might still, by a little ingenuity, gather the subdivisions from the text. Suppose you exercise your mind on this task! I shall suggest a lead for you in the first part:

I. THE GOOD SOLDIER. "I have fought the good fight."

A. The Christian warfare: "The good fight."

B. The apostle's struggle: "I have fought."

2. Sub-divisions may be gathered from other passages. We needed to do that in our outline on the *Conversion of a Preacher*. The PERSONAL WORKERS, Priscilla and Aquila, who taught Apollos the way of the Lord more perfectly, are named in the text, but what we know of their life story is told in other parts of the New Testament. Therefore we went to those other passages for our sub-divisions. You will often need to do that. Whenever a text suggests a topic of large interest it will be natural to seek other passages of Scripture to illustrate it.

3. The third source of sub-divisions in our outline was the inferences and implications of the text. We did not draw largely on that source; we did not need to, for the text was so rich itself. Very interesting discussions can be developed by working out the inferences of a text. As an example, consider Philippians 2:12b-13a, *"work out your own salvation with fear and trembling; for it is God who works in you, etc..."* As you meditate on this passage certain inferences will appear: (1) A man is responsible for his own salvation; (2) the fact that God concerns himself about us should be an incentive to us; (3) the matter of salvation calls for the most serious attention. This source of sub-divisions will become more available to you, probably, as you become experienced in sermon preparation.

4. A fourth source of sub-divisions may be found in an historical narrative to which the text relates. This was well illustrated in the development of outlines which was done under Plan No. 1. The texts Romans 4:3 and Hebrews 11:24-26, dealing with the faith of Abraham and Moses, were amplified by reference to the story of these men recorded in Genesis and Exodus (Chapter 2).

5. If the text contains a figure of speech, the figure used may suggest the sub-divisions. In Matthew 5:13-14 three figures are used. Your main divisions may use these – the salt, the light, the city. The text would supply some sub-divisions in the way suggested above. Others would be indicated by the figures employed, for instance, salt preserves, is tasty; light illuminates, gladdens, aids growth.

6. Sometimes--quite often, in fact--your subdivisions will be arguments or proofs to establish a position you are affirming, or duties that derive from the facts you present. Study the following outline:

CROWNED WITH LOVING-KINDNESS
(Psalm 103:4b)
I. The Goodness of God:

    A. Revealed in His Creation.

    B. Seen in Personal Blessings.

    C. Manifested in Jesus the Savior.

II. Its Effects on our Lives:

    A. Inspires our Gratitude: (1Kings 8:66)

    B. Rebukes our Sin: (Romans 2:4)

    C. Sustains us in Trial. (Psalm 27:13)

Sermon Titles

Another matter of importance in the work of sermon preparation is the selection of sermon titles. We have already stressed the value of imagination in the development of material.

Imagination is the hand-maid of reason in every part of sermonic work, and nowhere more so than in the discovery of arresting titles for sermons and main divisions. An experienced church elder gave me a valuable lesson here. I was preparing a sermon on that wondrously rich text for a gospel message, even though it is in the Old Testament (Isaiah 55:6-7). I made no effort to find a title for the sermon, but selected the first three words of the text, "Seek the Lord." The title was sent to the elder with a view to its being displayed in front of the church. He objected: "That's too ordinary, too trite. That subject won't grab anybody's attention." I set to work to find something better – I saw the value of the suggestion. The better title did not come readily. I consulted other ministers. I delayed the preaching of that sermon for weeks. I found a satisfactory title finally, I presume, for I preached the sermon, but I have forgotten what it was. I know what the results were, however. This provocative suggestion stirred within me the desire to find or create arresting and thought-provoking sermon titles. Years afterwards I was in a country town at an Endeavour Convention, and a country preacher, in greeting me in a convention meeting, said that though he had never met me, he felt that he knew me to a degree, for he had always been interested and intrigued by the sermon announcements appearing in the papers from week to week. The late Dr. Watson (Ian Maclaren) gave much attention to this matter, and is reported to have said that the framing or the finding of the title was almost as laborious as the writing of the sermon. You are to speak on Matthew 6:33, "*Seek first the Kingdom of God.*" You may entitle your sermon casually "The Kingdom of God," or "Seek first the Kingdom," but such titles will give you no advantage of anticipative attention on the part of possible hearers. In these days of priorities a much more suggestive title is "Priority No. 1."

Do not, I beg of you, manufacture fantastic or outrageous titles for your sermons with the object of arousing fabricated interest or creating a sensation.

Similar thought and care with the headings of the main divisions may do much to arouse interest in the sermon, for after all you must make it interesting. A sermon on Hebrews 3:12-14 may have the following title and divisions:

Title: FAITHFUL UNTO DEATH

> I. Holding Fast. "Hold the beginning… to the end."
>
> II. A Warning. "Exhort one another ... lest any of you be hardened," etc.
>
> III. An Exhortation: "Beware brethren," etc.

The apostle did not engage in carnal warfare, but he freely used the language of warfare, and in these days of conflict, surely a much better set out of this sermon outline is:

Title: FOR THE DURATION

Main Divisions:--
> I. The Terms of Enlistment
>
> II. The Danger of Desertion
>
> III. A Call to Attention

Propositional Outlines

It is not necessary always to design the outline in the form of titles. The headings may be statements or propositions. The late G. H. Morrison, of Glasgow, preached a great sermon on Jeremiah 9:2, 40:4-6. It was entitled *The Wish to Escape*, and after his introduction Dr. Morrison said: "*I shall divide what I have to say under these heads. First, We all feel sometimes the longing to escape. Second, this longing betrays itself in many ways. Third, The duty of the Christian is to crush it."*

I have sometimes found this propositional method very helpful when the work of preparation dragged. To say things about the text may be as helpful in its way as that of asking questions. The Outline on the Parable of the Treasure (Chapter 3) is of this nature. The publication, *Highland Shepherds*, by Dr. A. W. Hewitt, quotes a very interesting example of this method. The text was Matthew 14:9: *"And the king was sorry; nevertheless, because of the oaths and because of those who sat with him, he commanded IT to be given to HER."* The sermon was called *The Unroyal King*, and the outline as follows:

I. The thought of so great a sin made him sorry.

A. He paved his own way straight to the sin.

B. But it gave his conscience a fair challenge.

C. And made him desire to escape it.

II. But he was influenced by his past boasting.

A. He wished to be consistent with his past self.

B. In its worst part.

C. When consistency with God would have saved him.

III. And he was influenced by those who sat around him,

A. Who were his subjects and might have been influenced by him,

B. Who were watching to see this deed interpret his heart's religion,

C. While he had forgotten that among those who sat around him was God.

IV. And he committed the sin

A. Which was the inevitable result of his folly and weakness (II. and III.).

B. Which cut off a saving influence from those around him,

C. And which he could neither undo nor put out of his conscience forever.

The outline is unusual – nearly every line in it is a statement with a verb; the outline reads like a short story itself, but each line is a main division or a sub-division needing development.

In the study of sermon development by means of questions, we saw that questions may well be used as the main headings. (Plan No. 1, Chapter 2) In such a case the subdivisions answer the questions. The interrogative method may be used in other ways. The title may be a question, and the main divisions answer it. Fry, in *Elementary Homiletics*, gives this example:

Interrogative Outlines

WHY DID CHRIST WEEP OVER JERUSALEM? –Luke 19:41

Main Divisions:
   I. Because of its sin.

   II. Because of its unbelief.

   III. Because of its doom.

If the main divisions are titles, the sub-divisions may be in question form. Example: Hebrews 4:16: *"Let us therefore come boldly to the throne of grace, that we may obtain mercy and find grace to help in time of need."*

I. The invitation to prayer.

    A. What? "Let us...come."

    B. Where? "To the throne of grace."

    C. How? "Boldly"

II. The reasons for prayer.

    A. Why? "That we may obtain mercy and may find grace."

    B. When? "To help in time of need."

For Review:

1. Name the sources of sub-divisions. Discuss any other sources that may be used.

2. Find a good title for a sermon on Isaiah 55:6-7.

3. Put the main divisions of the sermon outline on Hebrews 3:12-14 into propositions.

4. What three uses of the interrogative method are suggested?

7. The Completed Outline

We are ready now to appreciate the complete outline, showing the various parts of a sermon, as they have been studied in the preceding chapters. This outline is not designed to be glanced at, or to be skimmed over lightly. Do you just time to read it through? Don't do it – lay it aside and pick up a short story. Leave the outline until you have time to study it thoroughly.

THE TITLE.

A GRACIOUS INVITATION.
The Text (which study) Revelation 22:17: *And the Spirit and the bride say, "Come!" And let him who hears say, "Come!" And let him who thirsts come. Whoever desires, let him take the water of life freely."*

Introduction: The text is among the closing words of the Bible. A gracious invitation among the last revealed words of Christ.

Theme: The gospel invitation is the call of Christ to man to come and satisfy the deepest needs of his being.

MAIN DIVISION I.

THE INVITATION.

"Come." "Take the water of life freely."
Sub-divisions--
>   A. Come—repeated three times.
>
>   B. Take--gifts must be accepted.
>
>   C. Water

Sub-sub-divisions--

    (a) Cleansing.

    (b) Cooling.

    (c) Refreshing.

    (d) Thirst-satisfying.

D. Of Life.

    (a) Spiritual satisfaction for the distressed.

    (b) Pardon for the sinful.

E. Freely.

MAIN DIVISION II.

THE HERALDS.

"The Spirit." "The Bride." "Him that hears."
Sub-divisions--

    A. The Spirit. How does the spirit invite?
    Sub-sub-divisions--
    (a) In the Word.

    (b) By the Church.

    (c) By his gracious influence

    B. The Bride--the Church--says Come.

    (a) By Preaching.

(b) By Personal Invitation.

(c) By her Beneficent Life.

C. All who hear repeat the invitation.

(a) It is a privilege so to do.

(b) It is a responsibility.

MAIN DIVISION III.

THE INVITED.

"Him who thirsts." "Whoever desires."
Sub-divisions--
    A. The Thirsty. Those who thirst
    Sub-sub-divisions--
    (a) For Pardon;

    (b) For Peace of Mind;

    (c) For fullness of Life.

    B. Whoever desires. The invitation is

    (a) Universal: "Whoever."

    (b) Requires Decision: "Desires."

Conclusion--

The gospel invitation is an expression of the loving heart of God, manifest in Christ. It is calculated to meet the deepest needs of the human heart. Respond to the call.

Be sure to study this outline carefully, painstakingly. Once you have thoroughly mastered the art, the preparation of sermons and addresses will become easy for you.

You will notice that the outline is a completely textual one. The main headings cover the whole of the message of the text, and they are all included in the text. (See rules for main divisions, Chapter 5)

Notice also that all the sub-divisions are from the text. Not many texts are so rich in material for subdivisions as this one. Still, a great deal depends on one's ability to discover sub-divisions. That will come by earnest practice.

The sub-sub-divisions are drawn from different sources. The first set, under "Water," is from the figure of speech used. The next two sub-divisions, under "Of Life," are implications. All the rest of the subdivisions are implied in or are applications of the text, except the last two, which are from the text itself. (Cf. Chapters 5 and 6)

You probably noticed that after each main heading a part of the text is quoted – the part of the text on which the main heading is based. It is a good habit to cultivate. As a result you will be able to determine readily if the main headings cover the whole of the text.

An outline is not a living thing. It is a skeleton. Just as the frame of the human body is designed to support tissue and nerves and blood vessels, and respond to life, so this outline, to become a sermon, must carry the message of the everlasting gospel, become alive with interest, and energized by the vitality of the preacher's soul. The body needs its skeleton, and dry enough work it is to learn its parts – the vertebrae, the humerus, the patella, the metacarpus – as all students of first-aid know. The sermon needs its outline too, and it is not an inspiring thing in itself – introduction, division, etc. God formed the human body and breathed into it the breath of life and man became a living soul. So we are to do the creative work of forming the sermon outline and breathe into it the breath of spiritual life. To this outline we bring on the great day of public opportunity a divine enthusiasm and sympathy and conviction and the will to move men to decision.

For Review:

1. Discuss material (concrete situations, illustrations, etc.) to amplify the sub-divisions in the above outline dealing with the water of life.

2. How could you make real to yourself and your congregation the offer of the gospel to those who thirst for peace of mind or the fullness of life?

8. Methods of Sermon Division

Earlier in this discussion we comforted our hearts with the admission of a critic that never in the world before was there a class commanding such a vast hearing as preachers enjoy. When, however, we compare the present state of affairs with that of an earlier day, we are bound to admit that we have lost ground terribly. Plenty of sermons are preached, but for the most part they are delivered to small groups of people. Dr. Harry Emerson Fosdick, who was one of the outstanding preachers of an earlier day, and regularly enjoyed the experience of preaching to multitudes, engaged himself with his less eminent brethren, and said that we need not be surprised at the revulsion against preaching because we have richly deserved it. We have preached too much and not well enough. Without doubt the preacher's task is taken too lightly by most preachers. Not many preachers will take their pulpit work seriously enough to build good sermons.

A number of years ago a "Colyum Conductor" in "The Churchman" (America) directed his shafts at the professional patter and stereotyped talk that so often passes for modern preaching. To illustrate the depths to which preachers may fall, this journalist offered to take any text and any topic that might be suggested, and fit them together in a sort of homily that passes muster in many a pulpit. His challenge was accepted, and he was given for a text, *"He (Benaiah) also had gone down and killed a lion in the midst of a pit on a snowy day."* (1 Chronicles 11:22), and a topic, *"The Dangers of Mah Jong."* He submitted the following outline: "Intro:: Modern generation seeks easy way. Follows fashion, like this silly one of Chinese game. It leads to gambling. Getting something for nothing. Bad principle. Benaiah a different sort. Lived in a heroic age. Had to fight for everything he got. Did not look for easy time. Actually went down into a pit. Fight not forced upon him. Notice that he fought: (I.) A lion. Smaller man would have chosen a dog or a cat. King of beasts. See encyclopedia. Quote poem with 'tawny mane', which we have forgotten. Choose hardest tasks. (II.) In a pit. No escape. Back to wall. Now or never. Do or die. This parish at a crisis. (III.) In a snowy day. We would have waited for the sunshine. The right time to do a worthwhile job is when everything is against us. Conclusion: Instead of wasting time in this silly fashion, and being led into the dangerous vice of gambling, be a fighter, select a worthy antagonist, be willing to meet him under the most unfavorable conditions and at the least favorable time. This parish needs you. Join the Parish Aid, which has been reduced to three members, and help them to raise money for the parish house sink. Join the Men's Club, now reduced to one, and help shingle the rectory garage. Take a Sunday School class, etc." (From "The Christian Century.") This homiletic squib, while it reveals a lively imagination in its composer – an indispensable factor in good preaching – illustrates the sort of twaddle that sometimes has to do service when preachers shirk the work involved in great preaching. A willingness to work, and to master the technique of sermon building, is essential. Whatever course of sermon preparation men of genius are able to follow, and however much capable men of large experience may seem to ignore the fundamentals of homiletics, it is essential for men of the rank and file, where you and I belong, to pay the necessary price by stern attention to the principles which underlie good preaching.

Methods of Sermon Division

Strictly speaking, there are only two methods of sermon division – the textual and the topical. In the textual method a text is taken and analyzed; in the topical a topic or subject is discussed. Expository sermons, which will be discussed later, are in reality textual in nature, because they deal more or less with the text of Scripture.

The textual method is one of analysis. That is to say, the text is analyzed, or separated, into its parts, so that they may be studied in relation to one another. If you analyze a flower, you may destroy it. Its beauty may all disappear when it is dissected. A text, like a flower, may appear very beautiful when seen as a whole. But, unlike a flower, a text when analyzed may be made to yield its truest beauty.

The outline presented in Chapter 3 on the Parable of the Hidden Treasure, was a textual one. Each main division was drawn from the text, and the main divisions covered all the text. The completed outline in Chapter 7 is still more completely textual, because both the main divisions and the sub-divisions were drawn from the text.

The topical method is the opposite of analysis. It is synthetical in its treatment. That is to say, it brings together from various sources any material that may aid in the presentation of the subject. There may be a text used, but often it is merely a motto text which suggests a topic. The outline on "The Meaning of Sin" in Chapter 3 is a topical one. A text was not taken and analyzed, but several texts on the subject of sin were brought together, and the outline developed from a comparison of them all.

In order to make the process of preparing textual and topical sermons quite clear, and also to illustrate the difference between the two, let us develop the two kinds of outline, using the same text for both. The text is Romans 14:17: *"For the kingdom of God is not eating and drinking, but righteousness and peace and joy in the Holy Spirit."*

We shall use the textual or analytical method first. We notice that the text falls naturally into two parts, each with a definite statement. We notice that each half is divisible into separate ideas. The Kingdom of God. What is meant by that? "Not eating and drinking." That clearly is a reference to the physical life. "Righteousness and peace and joy." These are qualities of mind and character. "In the Holy Spirit." The qualities are not simply those that belong to a natural development but are developed in relation to the spirit of God.

Analysis – Textual Method

We take the two parts of the text as the bases of our main divisions. We use the subsidiary ideas in the text as bases for sub-divisions. It may be necessary for adequate treatment to introduce other sources for sub-divisions. Analyzing the text, and setting it out in outline, we arrive at this result:

I. A WARNING AGAINST FALSE IDEAS OF THE KINGDOM.

"The kingdom of God is not eating and drinking."

    A. The Kingdom of God

        (a) The exercise of God's authority, and

        (b) The territory over which He reigns.

    B. Not eating and drinking.

    It is not primarily physical. (See Matt. 4:4)

II. THE NATURE OF THE KINGDOM OF GOD.

"But righteousness and peace and joy in the Holy Spirit."

A. The characteristics of the Kingdom.

    (a) Righteousness, both in relation to God and man;

    (b) Peace, the result of righteousness, both in society, nations, etc.

    (c) Joy, the crowning achievement.

B. The Source of Kingdom qualities In the Holy Spirit.

An excellent introduction to this sermon would be a reference to the discussion about the eating of meats, of which the text is a part. A good conclusion would be an exhortation to seek to be filled with the Spirit, that the fruit of the Spirit (Gal. 5:22) might be seen in our lives, and the kingdom of God thus be extended.

Synthesis – Topical Method

Now let us treat the text by the topical method, instead of the textual or analytical method. Instead of dissecting the text and examining it minutely, we treat it as a topic. The topic suggested by the text is. "The Kingdom of God is concerned with qualities of character." Stated in this way, it becomes a theme (cf. Chapter 4), and we may use the text in introducing that subject. In a topical sermon we may have no further use for the text. It has introduced our topic, and we are now free to gather from any source material that will help to develop our theme. The text may indeed be useful as an introduction, if we explain why the apostle made this suggestive statement. But we are not bound now to follow the text any further, as this is not a textual sermon.

If you have any acquaintance with the subject of the kingdom of God as presented in the New Testament, you might easily build up an entirely different outline on the same topic, for the Scripture is rich and full in its discussion of the reign of God in the hearts of men. Here, however, is a topical outline:

Text: Romans 14:17.

Introduction: As above, or if you prefer, a general statement of the varied aspects of the kingdom in the New Testament.

I. THE KINGDOM OF GOD.

A. The burden of the preaching of John the Baptist and Jesus. (Matt. 3:3; Matt. 4:17).

B. Jesus was always talking about the kingdom. (See Matthew 13).

C. Many parables are used to illustrate the kingdom.

D. The kingdom should be a primary consideration to us. (Matt. 6:33).

II. THE KINGDOM CALLS, FOR PERSONAL RIGHTEOUSNESS.

A. The simplicity of children. (Matt. 18:1-4).

B. The humble heart. (Matt. 5:3).

C. Salvation from wickedness. (Gal. 5:21).

D. Personal conduct. (Matt. 5:20).

III. THE SOCIAL DEMANDS OF THE KINGDOM.

A. Requires that the will of God be done in earth as in heaven. (Matt. 6:10).

B. Repentance must issue in social results in the kingdom. (Luke 3:3; Luke 3:10-14).

C. Its fundamental principle is love, which strikes at the ruthless competitive system, and at everything that oppresses and wrongs men.

Conclusion: A call to repentance. (See Matt. 3:2; Matt. 4:17.)

You will find that a textual sermon, while it must be textual in that the text is analyzed, and its main headings, at least, are all drawn from the text, may use the topical method for sub-divisions, if the text does not provide them, or for illustrations and other material for development. For example, a short text, 1 Timothy 1:15: *"Christ Jesus came into the world to save sinners"* is used for a textual sermon. An analysis reveals three parts:

I. Christ Jesus

II. Came into the world

III. To save sinners.

As an outline that meets the needs of a textual sermon – it is wholly from the text, and contains nothing that is not in the text. But when you come to supply the sub-divisions, and to develop the subject, you must gather the materials from other sources, and thus you introduce something of the topical method.

For Review:

1. Supply sub-divisions for the above outline on 1 Timothy 1:15.

2. Use 1 Timothy 1:15 as a theme, and find main divisions for a topical sermon on that subject.

9. Topical Sermons

My experience with young men through the years tells me that many of them by this time are irked by this insistent demand to work out intricate outlines according to precise forms. They have known a few preachers – outstanding men, some of them who do not seem to worry about these finicky details. Which is probably true. They have also known of brilliant pianists who, so far as their public performances reveal it, do not have to worry about five-finger exercises. They have seen capable typists at work in city offices who do not have to worry about the use of their fingers on the machine, who indeed look neither at their fingers nor the machine. They also know, probably, some people who are not good pianists, who began to study music and hated the five-finger exercises, and did not persevere. They know typists – they may be among the number who could not be bothered to master the touch system on the typewriter, and who will be muddling typists all their lives. And with regard to preaching, the same principles are eternally true, except in the case of geniuses, and this book is not written for them. Even men who come to great distinction in music never get away from painstaking drill.

Drill

Paderewski said that if he stopped practicing at the piano one day he noticed the difference, if he stopped two days his family noticed it, three days and his friends were aware of the difference, and if he stopped for a week the musical world noticed the difference. It is likely that behind much great preaching there is much meticulous drill in sermon preparation which the public does not see and the uninitiated do not realize, so let us to work to master our technique. "Enter ye in by the strait gate, for wide is the gate and broad is the way that leads to dull and ineffective preaching, and many be they that enter in thereby. For narrow is the gate and straitened the way that leads to great preaching such as people in these fastidious days are willing to listen to, and few be they that find it." A modern translation, you will recognize, and I doubt if we should use versions in modern English too much in our pulpit work, though they have their uses.

Texts for Topical Sermons

We have now formed a very good idea of the nature of the topical sermon, but it will be well for us to realize the variety of subjects that will call for treatment in this way. Some of them are definitely related to texts. As examples, examine these:

1. Parallel passages expressing one idea. For instance, Psalm 103:12, *"As far as the east is from the west,* so *far has He removed our transgressions from us."* You may analyze it, textually, of course, but you would not get very far in the sermon by a geographical discussion of the distance of the east from the west. It is far better to treat it as a great statement of God's pardoning love – that is, as a topic, and bring to it all your resources of knowledge and experience of that great theme.

2. Short texts, like "Jesus Wept," "God is Light," may be better treated topically than textually. They are capable of textual treatment, of course, as in the following outline, which will serve for either text: (1) The Person Mentioned; (2) The Fact Declared. That is very trite, and ordinary, as is shown by the fact that it suits either text equally well. The sermons would be richer if you treated them as topics: *The Sympathy of Christ,* and *The Light of God.*

3. Great texts, rich and full of teaching, which would lend themselves fully for textual treatment, may yet sometimes be better treated as a topic. Perhaps in this case it is more common to select the topic first, and you seek a picturesque text to introduce it, and to remain as a permanent seed thought. You are to speak on "God's Wonderful Love" as it has been revealed to you in your experience of His grace, and John 3:16 may be your text, not only a motto text for a topical sermon, but the highlight of your presentation.

Subjects for Topical Doctrine

The extensive range of Christian, and the wide-reaching Sermons privileges, duties and perils of the Christian Life, offer themselves as topics. We must preach on these subjects, for this is an ignorant age concerning the content of the Christian faith. You will do well to preach on the principal doctrines, and proclaim your convictions concerning the Word of God, the Fatherhood of God, the Savior Christ Jesus, the Holy Spirit the Comforter, Man, Sin, Salvation, and the Future Hope. There are the festivals of the Church year – Easter, Thanksgiving, Christmas. There are the rich experiences of the Christian life – cleansing, guidance, adventure, fellowship. Time would fail to indicate the extent of the topics which offer themselves to our eager minds. We need never be at a loss for a theme.

No, our burden will not be the lack of a subject, but of a living approach to it. A textbook written in the days when preaching was a simpler proposition than it is now suggested the following type of outlines for such subjects as we have in mind:

I., Its Meaning; II., Its Proofs; III., Its Effects.

I., Its Lines; II., Its Limitations; III., Its Lessons.

I., The Duty Explained; II., Exemplified; III., Enforced.

Probably that kind of thing may still go over once or twice, but it is a pedestrian movement introduced where we need to mount up with wings as eagles. True, we must walk before we can fly, and it may be that in the beginning you cannot improve on the formal approach suggested. But keep your mind alert for the more vital approach. You want to speak on Christ and what he means to the world. Dr. Jowett had a sermon on "*If Christ had not Come,*" pointing out the alternatives – what our situation would be in such a case. J. Fort Newton once used a sentence in a sermon which arrested me immediately. I quote from memory, but he spoke of Paul as walking down the corridors of time turning out the lights of faith. That was Paul's way of showing how valuable faith is. "*If Christ is not risen, then our preaching is empty and your faith is also empty…if Christ is not risen, your faith is futile; you are still in your   sins!*" That sentence gave me a sermon on the essential nature of faith. In all your study you need to be on the watch for the striking phrase, the arresting thought – some living word that will give you an idea and an inspiration in preaching the great doctrines of the gospel.

Bible personalities often make peculiarly interesting topics for the presentation of a message. You may, as we found in examining Hebrews 11:24-26, discover a text that by analysis will give you the most significant portions of a man's life. Only rarely, however, will you find single texts that do more than suggest a single line of thought on such a subject, and you must therefore use the synthetic or topical method of treatment. You are attracted by the life of Abraham, and you seek a way to handle it. You examine with the aid of your concordance the word "Abraham." You come to Isaiah 41:8,

"Abraham my Friend." You go on to James 2:23, where the apostle, speaking of the patriarch, says: *"He was called the friend of God."* Dr. Alexander Maclaren had a sermon on that subject, and he outlined it with a number of affirmations which were illustrated by Abraham's relationship with God:

I. Friends trust and love one another.

II. Friends have frank, familiar interaction with one another.

III. Friends delight to meet each other's wishes.

IV. Friends give gifts to each other.

V. Friends stand up for each other.

If you know the life of Abraham (and you must know the life stories of these men if you would preach about them) you will see how simply it was done, and how beautiful a survey of the life of Abraham it is.

I have found that students as a rule prefer to preach topical rather than textual sermons. The reason no doubt is that a topic gives more freedom and provides more scope for the use of the stored resources of knowledge that one may have. I insist with my students that a certain proportion of their sermons, during their college days, must be textual – I would not do them the disservice of permitting them to imagine that the meanderings of their immature minds could ever be a complete substitute for the diligent painstaking analysis of a great passage of Scripture. Even the textual sermon will need the stored treasures of the mind to clarify and apply it, and this matter of acquiring useable material for sermon making is a very important one.

"How long should we spend in the preparation of a sermon each week?" asked a student this week. That depends. There are subjects already more or less mature in your minds, upon

which an hour or two of good solid work will produce a good result. Others that are new to your habits of thought will need many hours of study before they are ready for the pulpit. This is important, however: while you are preparing your next Sunday's sermon you are also preparing for sermons to be preached ten or twenty years down the road. And that not merely because you are informing your mind, but because you are definitely registering articles, illustrations, quotations, etc., which will be made available in the future by some sensible method of reference. You may use scissors and paste, and compile a scrap book. You may use separate large envelopes for different subjects, as D. L. Moody did. Better still, you may use a box file, properly indexed, to hold all the scrap material you think may have a future use.

The Permanent Notebook

[Editor: The following information concerning compiling a notebook is still true in principle, even though most of you reading this will have access to a computer and the internet, which takes away any limits to what resources you can gather and store.]

You will also find much material in books which you cannot deface, and so you must record in some other way. Here comes the notebook, one of the most useful articles in a preacher's study. If a fire should destroy my own study, my greatest loss would be the records and references compiled through many years, which give me ready access to a vast variety of subjects. This is the way it grows.

You secure a notebook sufficiently large to contain all the references you are likely to make for many years, and sufficiently well bound to endure years of careful handling. You keep it on your desk, ready for use. You are preparing a sermon, let us say, on the power of Christ in the world, and you are perusing E. Stanley Jones's "*The Christ of the Indian Road*" for information. You come to this statement:

"*Now the cross never knows defeat, for it is itself Defeat, and you cannot defeat Defeat. You cannot break Brokenness. It starts with defeat and accepts that as a way of life.*"

You say, "*That is a striking thought. I will be preaching on The Cross someday, and I'll want that reference.*" You take your thumb-indexed notebook and pencil, and under "C" you write a title, "The Cross." Under that you write "The Cross never knows defeat. Stanley Jones. 189, 55." The figures mean, first the number of the book in your library (for you, number your books for ready reference: 189 is the number of this book in my own library) and the page of reference. A few days later you read an arresting article on "The Last Full Measure." It has to do with the Cross. You put it in your box file (in my file it happens to be the 68th clipping under "P"). In your notebook you make this entry "The Cross": The Last Full Measure. File P, 68.

You must not make heavy work of the compilation of your notebook – it just grows, reference by reference. You will not try to think up a lot of subjects upon which you hope you will be able to compile references. You wait till something strikes you which you would like to keep, and you give it a title, and record the reference.

The first reference in my notebook under the title "Christ" is simply Book 2, 89 A.B. The reference is to a scrap book which I began to compile about forty years ago. (The scrap book method has long been abandoned for the more adaptable box file, but the old scrap books are kept). In years to come you will have thousands of references. Many of them you will have forgotten altogether, except as they may be registered in your unconscious mind where you cannot reach them. But through your notebook you will reach them, and you will bless the patient diligence which through the years provided you with such a fund of rich sermonic material.

For Review:

Prepare sermon outlines, one textual and the other topical, using Acts 17:30 as a text.

10. Expository Sermons

The preacher is first of all a teacher. It is his duty to make known the Word of God in such a way as to form correct habits of thought, conduct and worship. A rather interesting text is the marginal reading in the revised version of Daniel 12:3: *"The teachers shall shine as the brightness of the firmament."* We shall now turn our attention to expository preaching.

You will remember it was said that there are but two kinds of sermons, textual and topical. We have studied those two forms of sermon building. Every sermon is or should be an effort to interpret and apply the Word of God. The textual sermon analyzes and presents the substance of a definite text. The topical sermon employs a topic (a scriptural topic if it is preaching) and deals with it in the light of the general teaching of the Scriptures. Expository sermons are more directly related to the textual than to the topical sermons, although the truth of that statement may be affected by the method of the expositor. My friend of University days, the late H. E. Knott, M.A., in his book on expository preaching, made a comparison of the methods of two world famed expositors, G. Campbell Morgan and Alexander Maclaren. The former, he said, habitually took a phrase from a section or verse of Scripture and treated it somewhat as a topic, while the latter dealt with his section of Scripture in a more analytical way.

Probably it is true to say that expository preaching is the most difficult type of preaching, and at the same time it is more needed than any other. There is a lamentable ignorance of the Bible today. A very small percentage even of those who regularly attend church services have any useful knowledge of the Scriptures. The reason is that few people now read the Book regularly and constructively. A secondary reason, so far as church attendants are concerned, is that preachers have not done the work of exposition to a profitable extent. Exposition, as the word suggests, opens up the Scriptures, displays their meaning, reveals their matter, and vitalizes their message. It is a real art. It demands skill. A true expositor will understand his text-book, he will have insight into its depths, he will understand the psychology of his congregation, he will be aware of what is going on in the world, and he will seek to apply the Word of God to the lives of his people. "Who is sufficient for these things?" We qualify by our possession of the gifts of reason and imagination steeped in hard work and sanctified by the Spirit of God.

There are many questions of Biblical and Historical Criticism in these later days which are of immense importance in the work of exposition. The more the expositor knows of such subjects the better. But he must be careful not to confuse the average people, untrained to form their judgments on the historical and critical questions at issue, by forcing these questions upon them in his sermons. Such questions have little to do with the essential revelation and inspiration which make Bible exposition and application dynamic.

The advantages of expository preaching are these:

1. It brings preacher and hearer into direct contact with the mind of the Spirit.

2. It promotes the biblical knowledge of the preacher and the hearer.

3. It presents a comprehensive intelligent view of the revelation of God.

4. It opens up new ways of preaching truths that must be dealt with by the preacher again and again.

5. It enables a preacher to handle naturally, some subjects from which he would otherwise shrink. When they come in the course of regular expository studies they do not appear to be specially selected, though they may deal with living issues.

Definition of Expository Preaching

Perhaps now we are ready for a definition of expository preaching. Expository preaching is the consecutive treatment of some book, or extended portion of Scripture, or a single verse, in an effort to explain it, and apply it to life.

Expository preaching then is marked by three features:

1. It takes for its text a connected passage (more than a clause or a verse generally), a psalm, a parable, an argument or portion of an argument, a scene or narrative, etc.

2. It expands the meaning of the passage in a clear and forcible way.

3. It applies its lessons to life.

There are different methods of expository preaching, and some which were acceptable once upon a time, when Alice was in Wonderland, that cannot be used to advantage now.

For example, *The Running Commentary*. Dr. R. W. Dale, celebrated British preacher of a generation ago, speaking of his own expository sermons, said that he carefully "explained and illustrated, clause by clause, verse by verse, a group of chapters, or a complete book of Holy Scripture." That kind of exposition, however, has long ceased to be acceptable to listeners. Some few dear saintly souls, to whom the Word is the very breath of life, may be delighted to hear it yet, and to such folk, in some small Bible study group, you may even yet dare to do it. Dr. James Black tells of a preacher whom he heard when he was a child, who started in to expound the epistle to the Philippians. Dr. Black said: "We loved the man for many things, but in the end we hated the book of Philippians." The preacher died after a year and ten months, and he was only in the middle of the second chapter. To go through a book verse by verse, or phrase by phrase, plodding unweariedly and wearyingly on, is not exposition for today. Exit The Running Commentary!

I have said that the work of exposition is more related to textual than to topical preaching. Some forms, however, are distinctly topical. A biblical character study, the sketching of a portrait, the setting out of the striking characteristics of a personality – psychological, moral and religious – is a very helpful form of exposition. Dr. George Matheson's *Representative Men of the Bible* are good examples. So, too, is the work of verbal dramatization, a field where a preacher with an imaginative gift and dramatic powers may find wide scope for his talents. Who has not felt the dramatic interest of the story of Naaman the leper, or of the incident of Elijah and the priests of Baal! There are numerous incidents, as well as dramatic words and phrases, which lend themselves to this kind of treatment. The preacher who announced as his subject, "A King Pursues a Flea" (1 Samuel 24:14), had an eye for a dramatic situation.

Types of Exposition

The usual forms of exposition are:

1. The exposition of a selected portion of Scripture;

2. The study of related passages;

3. The message of a book, when such book is taken as a whole.

4. The continuous exposition of a book in a series of sermons.

In expounding an extended section of Scripture, attention to some important principles will be of, value.

First, every phrase or idea in the passage does not require treatment. It would be impossible to deal with them all, and the ability to make a selection of relevant details is important.

Second, leading ideas in the passage may be selected, around which the general teaching of the lesson may be gathered.

Third, the lesson must be a vital one; it must have relation to life.

Fourth, the exposition must be interesting. This should be included as a matter of course in the last statement, but unfortunately it does not follow that everything that has a vital relation to life is interesting to people. Religion, for instance! Some people are more interested in a football game! Therefore, if a vital subject is not naturally interesting, you must make it so by your manner of handling it.

Leading Ideas for Exposition

We come then to the exposition of a selected portion of Scripture. It is Ephesians 4:1-5:21. Read it! It is a long passage and it is full of rich material for exposition. Did you notice that a certain word, "Walk," occurs again and again (4:1; 4:17; 5:2; 5:8; 5:15)? It seems as if all the counsel in the mind of the apostle was gathered around the way a Christian walked, in a figurative sense, of course.

"Walk worthy of the calling with which you were called, etc..." What ideas were in his mind there? What is the calling, and what "walk" would be worthy of it? Only today I saw walking

along a city street, a woman who was drunk and disorderly. Her face was marked with bruises, and she was shouting foolish inanities as she walked. She was not walking worthily of her womanhood.

"I say...that you should no longer walk as the rest of the Gentiles walk, in the futility of their mind, etc." What things are to be avoided in the Christian life? Paul tells us in vv. 18-20. There was a real difference between Christians and Gentiles in those days.

"Walk in love, as Christ also has loved us, etc." What kind of a walk will that be? Remember you find out from the context in each case, because you are expounding Scripture. The first thing about Christ is his sacrifice (5:2).

"Walk as children of light." That is a beautiful phrase; what can it mean? Your context will tell you, and that is where you need to go for the work of exposition. On the positive side *"goodness, righteousness, and truth, finding out what is acceptable to the Lord"*; and on the negative side *"have no fellowship with the unfruitful works of darkness,"* the things which it is *"shameful even to speak of"* (vv. 9-12). In this connection notice this striking statement: *"All things that are exposed are made manifest by the light"* (v. 13). Is this a reference to the way a wholesome character by its very beauty reveals by contrast what is selfish and mean in others?

"See then that you walk circumspectly." That could be a general exhortation covering all the rest, but the apostle does not mean it that way, and the context again presents us with definite ideas concerning conduct.

These five passages are related to practically all that the apostle says in this long section, and they are all expressed in a figure of speech. By the time we have surrounded these passages with the ideas in Paul's mind, the exposition will certainly be profitable if we can make it interesting. It should be interesting. Both the kind of life the writer has in mind, and the metaphor he uses, are interesting. Have you noticed how differently men walk? Some go with choppy steps, some slouch, some shuffle, some walk firmly, or brightly. Granted that feet and limbs are in good condition, a man's walk shows character. Well, there's an introduction. "Watch your step" may be a good title. Under the figure of walking we are to study how a Christian should conduct himself – there is the theme.

Exhaustive Study

Now for the outline. We must study our passage more before we are ready for that. We cannot expound a scripture portion that we have not thoroughly studied. Don't forget – this is no lazy man's job. One of the verses around which our study centers is expressed negatively – there is a kind of walking we must not do (4:17). It is often well to deal with negative points of view first, in order to leave your positive elements for the conclusion. Here then is the first main division. The apostle was much concerned about sexual impurity here (4:19; 5:3). These Ephesians must have been a loose crowd once. We were never as bad as that, perhaps. Or perhaps we were. In imagination anyway! (4:18). Or loose talk! (5:4). They had been thieves, some of them (4:28). There was lying too (4:25), and bitterness and anger and evil speaking and malice (4:31). The lightning may be striking close now!

"Walk worthy of the calling." Here is the second main division. A great vocation, this Christian life! What can be worthy of it? The particular thing (though there are others) that Paul has in mind here is a striving after unity. *"Endeavoring to keep the unity of the Spirit"* (4:3). *"Till we all come to the unity of the faith"*

(4:13). *"Speaking truth in love"* (4:15).

"Walk as children of light." Third main division! The apostle is drawing on his imagination here, but we can follow. What does light do? It shows things up when they need to be exposed (5:13). Its very presence is a rebuke to evil (5:11). It stands for all that is good and righteous and true (5:9), as contrasted with the unfruitful works of darkness (5:9-12). *"See then that you walk circumspectly"* (5:15). The "walk" again! Shall we make this another main division? It is the positive side of the first leading idea we had; perhaps we could include it there, when we come to prepare our outline. But of course it could be made another main point if it appealed to us that way. Perhaps it should be given a particular emphasis, because many Christians are not careful how they walk.

Here is the next great thought: *"Walk in love"* (5.2). That is a main division for sure. The new commandment and the greatest of all commandments! What kind of walk is this? *"Be kind ... tenderhearted, forgiving ... just as God"* (4:32). Imitators of God in everything (5:1). Loving as Christ did (5:2).

Thus we have gathered in a somewhat ordered way the leading thoughts of this great passage. We must now set it out in outline form, for although we are preparing an exposition of a portion of Scripture, a definite outline, with suggestive main headings, a comprehensive analysis will help both our hearers and ourselves. Even so, it is but an outline of the teaching of the Scripture which we are expounding. The sermon will still need your pertinent illustration and definite application to life.

Outline of Exposition

The following outline covers the essential details that our study of the passage has revealed.

WATCH YOUR STEP!
Ephesians 4:1-5:21

Introduction: The apostle was interested in the way men walk. How differently they do it! Illustrate. A man's walk may reveal his character.

I. FORBIDDEN PATHS. "No longer walk as the rest of the Gentiles walk" (4:17).

Their stumbling gait is

    A. Due to:

        (a) A perverted mind (4:18).

        (b) A hard heart (4:18).

    B. And results in:

        (a) Immorality (4:19).

        (b) Thieving (4:28).

        (c) Lying (4:25).

        (d) Bitterness (4:31).

II. THE AVENUE OF HONOR. "Walk worthy of the calling with which you were called" (4:1).

A worthy walk is characterized by

A. A Humble Spirit (4:2).

B. Longsuffering and Forbearance. (4:2).

C. Diligence to keep the Unity of the Spirit. (4:3).

D. Aspiration towards Unity of the Faith. (4:13).

E. Desire for Completeness in Christ (4:14-16).

III. THE WAY OF LIGHT. "Walk as Children of Light" (5:8).

The function of light

A. It is revealing (5:13).

B. It is convicting (5:13).

C. It produces fruit (5:9) of goodness.

D. But not the unfruitful works of darkness (5:11).

IV. A DIFFICULT TRACK. "Walk circumspectly" (5:15).

A. Danger of indolence in evil times (5:16).

B. A call for the exercise of common sense. (5:17).

C. Pitfalls on the road (5:18).

D. Power for the way (5:18-19).

V. THE KING'S HIGHWAY. "Walk in love, as Christ also has loved" (5:2).

It is:

A. A way of sacrifice (5:2).

B. A way of goodness (5:3-4a).

C. A way of gratitude (5:4b).

Conclusion: The call of the Christian life to great character. The wide range of evil to be avoided, and the life comprehending simple goodness in every form is here set forth. A word of exhortation and appeal.

For Review:

1. Discuss the extent to which expository preaching draws upon both the textual and topical methods of sermon preparation.

2. Under what conditions might the running commentary be used? (The notes suggest one – are there others?)

3. Following the study of Ephesians 4:1-5:21, prepare an independent outline covering the results of your study.

11. Expository Sermons (Continued)

Exposition of Related Passages

The study of related passages. This is the second suggested form of expository preaching. It is often a profitable practice to compare scripture with scripture, and thus establish or illustrate some doctrine or truth that needs emphasis. You may remember that Paul in Romans 4:24, in stressing the doctrine that justification is by faith and not by works, illustrates his point by reference to Abraham, and quotes the passage, Abraham believed God and it was *"accounted to him for righteousness."* The author of James, however, sets out to prove that a man is justified by works and not by faith alone, and he also illustrates his point by reference to Abraham, and quotes the very same text to prove it. The apparent divergence seemed to Luther to be so great that for a while he would not admit James as of the same canonical value as Romans. However, there is really no discrepancy, as you will know, or if not, you can readily discover it by consulting some good commentaries, and the study of these related passages, and of the doctrine of faith and works, would provide you with excellent material for an exposition.

The Plan No. 3 for sermon construction, described in Chapter 3, is really an exposition of related texts. When you select more extended passages which are related to one another, you will be on an expositor's happy hunting ground. The parables of the kingdom in Matthew 13 are all related, because they have all to do with the kingdom, and because they present different aspects of the kingdom they are very interesting for comparative studies.

Exposition of a Book

The message of a book as a whole is another profitable subject for expository preaching. The book of Jonah – do you know the message of the book of Jonah? There are lots of people who think that Jonah is merely the story of a whale who swallowed a man. *"This is the tragedy of the book of Jonah,"* one writer has said, *"that a book which is made the means of one of the most sublime revelations of truth in the Old Testament, should be known to most only by its connection with a whale."* The book presents a prophet of God, narrow, prejudiced, exclusive, revengeful, who is a bigger heathen than the heathen sailors on his ship – at any rate, he was the only man who had no God to pray to in an emergency. It shows a Jew – one of God's elect race who had none of God's love for the heathen, and would gladly have consigned them all to death.

More than any book in the Old Testament, this book reveals God's universal love, and how inadequate were the exclusive ideas of the Jews to represent the fatherly love of God for all His creatures.

Well now, you are to preach an expository sermon on the book of Jonah. You read it, and read it again. You consult some good commentaries. You employ the threefold combination which, alone, as I have told you, can unlock the secrets of good preaching: diligent thought, a gift of imagination, and hard work, and the greatest of these is hard work. (You will not be foolish enough to suppose that by imagination I mean mere fancy which invents unrealities – it is the gift by which you reproduce the life and times of Jonah's day, the men, the scenes and the situations described.)

You will see that the book of Jonah is a noble attempt to help Jews to see the folly and sin of their narrow exclusiveness, and the desire of God to include even the heathen in the sweep of His love. In those days a Jew did not as a rule feel that God's grace could be extended to the Gentiles. They were fit only for punishment and extermination. Through this little book God is teaching His people that He cares for the heathen too, and that they are susceptible to the call to repentance, and are eligible for salvation. Yes, the Old Testament revelation reaches its high-water mark in this little book. It will provide you with an excellent expository sermon, one which people will listen to if you are any good at all. Tell the story first, and then set out the great lessons. And please do not tell any foolish story about Jonah and the whale, in a silly attempt to be funny. Treat the whole story with the reverence it deserves – whatever may be your particular view of that particular event – and help your people to understand this early lesson of the universal love of God.

Many of the books of the Bible will be available for expository treatment in this way.

The fourth form of exposition suggested is the continuous exposition of a book in a series of sermons. I need not do more than make a few suggestions on the way of approach to this work. You will never cease to remember that in expository work especially the matter must be vital and living, the presentation vivid and interesting, demanding that the preacher prepare himself with diligence.

Continuous Exposition

In presenting the message of any book, in one sermon or a series of sermons, you will need to study the personality and history of the author, the literary form of the book, the purpose of the author, and how he works it out. Necessarily you will make yourself acquainted with the contents of the book, and you will seek the most effective way of handling it.

(a) You may select the chief subjects with which the book deals, and discuss them in order, seeking to give them a living interest to your hearers. The epistle of James is a very practical one. He discusses such subjects as temptation, salvation by works, pretension, purity, God's providence and faith-healing. These are up-to-date enough in all conscience. He says things calculated to make rich people squirm, and to make the scandal-mongers "hair to stare," as Shakespeare says.

(b) A series of sermons tracing the progress of the gospel in the first days of Christianity could be made of compelling interest, on condition that you made yourself acquainted with your subject. You probably know the book of Acts already as well as any in the Bible, and that may be your peril. Read it again, and master a good outline of the book such as is found in R. B. Rackham's commentary on the Acts of the Apostles; read through Farrar's Early Days of Christianity, and Conybeare and Howson's Life and Epistles of St. Paul, and you will be ready to begin the specific study in the preparation of the sermons themselves. You will find it an enriching task, and the chances are that you will have interested hearers.

(c) The books of the prophets are rich fields for the expositor's research work. Amos, for instance, is full of stinging rebuke of a people for its national follies. Dr. James Black suggests that we expound this book by its vices. "For modern political cleansing, and the teaching of God about national righteousness, could you have a finer setting than this prophet's mission? Take his message under the sins which he scourges, and show the remedies of a true religion-national greed and selfishness, the oppression of the poor, faithless living, the fallacy and tragedy of apparent prosperity, the penalty of luxury, the decay of public virtue, and the appearance without the reality of religion. If you desire to speak to the modern man about national purity, can you have a finer platform? Under a scheme like that you may unfold the robust message of Amos and relate it clearly to our worried life and our worrying problems." (The Mystery of Preaching, p. 130.)

(d) You may find a series on the life of Christ a rewarding course of study. You will use the four Gospels as your source of information. This will seem to be a formidable bit of work, and you certainly need to study the background of the gospels as well as the books themselves. I once preached a series of forty-two sermons covering some of this ground. There were six sermons on each of the following subjects: The Wondrous Life of Jesus; Great Moments in Jesus' Life; The Great Parables of Jesus; The Great Miracles of Jesus; The Great Messages of Jesus; The Great Themes of Jesus, and Jesus in the Life of Today. Only men in a settled ministry could attempt such a work as that. I think that the preachers most qualified to judge would say such a series is too long, and so it is, unless you are prepared to perform a herculean task to carry it through successfully. My experience has been that a regular audience is improved in numbers, sometimes very much so, by a solid series of sermons faithfully presented.

The suggestion thus given may be extended in a variety of ways. Avoid sameness. You may be tempted to treat the next book as you had treated the last. Better wait until you discover a new line of approach – find a succession of problems discussed, or personalities portrayed, or events described. Your previous studies have taught you how to construct a sermon-the main principles are the same for every type of sermon. If you wish to excel in this type of work you will discipline yourself in the exercise of the principles which govern it.

For Review:

1. Suggest a line of study based on related passages which unfold some doctrine or Christian duty.

2. Suggest a unified series of sermons based on Genesis 1 to 9.

12. Illustrating the Sermon

If you have taken the work of "exposing" a passage of Scripture (such as the exposition of Ephesians 4:1-5:21) seriously, you realize that the work of preparation is heavy going. You will sense the fact also that the task of delivering the results of your study to a congregation is no light one. A preacher could easily be heavy and dull with such a subject.

He need not be; he can make it interesting. That is part of his business as a preacher – not merely to touch lightly some of the more readily accessible passages of the Word of God, but to display the treasures which are hidden in the depths. No doubt most preachers have avoided this responsible duty to a large degree. Is it because we dislike the hard work involved, or that we feel unequal to the task?

Let us turn back to our exposition. It is full of essential truth. Essential truth is not always interesting – we must make it so. In so far as we can show that it is a vital message, directly concerned with the lives people live, it will be full of interest. Almost always, in this age, when people's interests are not chiefly in the most important things of life, we shall need to resort to such expedients as are available for preachers in securing the attention of the hearers.

The Art of Illustration

The art of illustration is one that all preachers need to develop. The word itself is a metaphor – it means to make lustrous, to throw light upon, a subject. In the preparation of every part of a sermon, a preacher should not be concerned only with the intellectual satisfaction he himself finds in its outworking. He should ask. Will this be interesting to my people? Can I make this live? One of the surest ways to do this is to discover or create good illustrations.

The first main division of our exposition was "Forbidden Paths." Can we illustrate that? There comes to my mind a story told by F. W. Boreham (the reading of whose works, by the way, would be as good as a university course in the art of illustration) of the old gardener of Versailles, who was distressed because the courtiers from the palace constantly tramped over his flower beds and ruthlessly destroyed his seedlings. He went to the king, Louis the Fourteenth, and confided his trouble to his royal master. The king ordered that little tablets – "etiquette" – be neatly arranged along the sides of the flower beds, and a state order was issued ordering all his courtiers to walk carefully within the etiquette. "And so the poor old gardener not only protected the flowers that he loved from the pitiless feet of the high-born vandals, but he enriched our vocabulary with a new and startlingly significant word. The art of life consists in keeping carefully within the ways marked out by the etiquette." Now that is a first-class illustration of the idea emphasized in the first part of our exposition. You may say it is not easy to drop on such illustrations when you want them. No, it is not. I searched for a long time trying to get a fully satisfactory illustration for that section, and it came to me at last. You must not be afraid of work if you want to preach helpful and interesting sermons.

Come now to the second main division of the sermon. The Avenue of Honor--"walk worthy of the calling." In our exposition notes an illustration has already been given. I find many illustrations come to me from recent experiences, and they perhaps are the most serviceable of all. The third division of the sermon, The Way of Light, is sufficiently illustrated by the metaphor itself, and the use we made of it – we could hardly fail to be interesting there. You will not find it hard to select a suitable illustration for the next division, A Difficult

Track: "See then that you walk circumspectly." You may know what it is to pick a track carefully over precipitous mountain paths. Personally I always look carefully how I walk over damp stones in a creek bed or valley, because once, years ago, when I was walking with preachers over the rocks near Sherbrook Falls, I slipped, and the resulting fall necessitated a visit to a surgeon.

When you come to The King's Highway, *"Walk in love, as Christ also has loved us,"* the last section of the sermon, it will not be difficult to select a suitable illustration. The essential thought in the text is that of sacrifice – Christ's sacrifice. The other day the papers told of a fire in a hall at Warburton, in which a large number of people were in peril. When most of the company had escaped, a Seventh Day Adventist pastor saw two women, one of them with a baby, in a precarious position. He rushed to the rescue, and as he passed the room where the picture films were stored an explosion took place, and he was badly burned. In spite of his injuries, he went on with his mission, and took the child, and dropped it through a window to the outstretched arms of friends twelve feet below. He risked his own life, and was seriously injured, in his work of rescue – the deed of a true pastor of the flock. During the pneumonic influenza epidemic many years ago, when many families were unable to secure help in their distress, the mayor of the city in which I lived sought for volunteers. I phoned him to ask why he did not approach the churches – it was their business to help in such emergencies. He rather scoffed at the idea that help could be had from that source, and I undertook to get him some. I found several women who were prepared to go into the stricken homes, risking their own lives, to care for the sick. These are the kind of people who walk the King's Highway – the way of love.

Illustrations such as these not only make clear in a practical way the meaning of the passage you are expounding; they also give the human touch that lends immediate interest to the ancient word of instruction. The work of illustration must not be overdone. On a dull day you may need to pull up all the blinds in the room, but there are days when the lifting of too many blinds will produce an uncomfortable glare. There are perhaps some sermons that are of a nature to need many illustrations, but one effective illustration is usually enough for any particular lesson you are emphasizing. There are quite a number of illustrations – parables – used by our Lord in the seventh chapter of Matthew to set forth various aspects of the kingdom. They were probably not all in one sermon, however; it is generally thought that the gospel writer compiled them from different sources. Even if they were all spoken at one time, they illustrate different aspects of the kingdom and so are in order.

Famed Preachers

It is good, when we are learning how to do things, to see how they are done by the masters. Great preachers use illustrations effectively. I glanced up at my book shelves when I came to this point, thinking that I would illustrate the art of illustration by showing how world-renowned preachers did it. Whom should I choose? Gossip, Fosdick, Morrison, Drummond, Jones, Robertson, Black – any one of them would do. I took down Henry Drummond. His sermon, *The Kingdom of God and Your Part in it,* has this fine illustration, which completely reveals his essential message.

"Let me tell you of the work of some university men in the city of London. They went to a district in the East End – a God-forsaken and sunken place, occupied for miles entirely by working people. They rented a house and became known as settlers in that poor district. They gave themselves no air of superiority. They did not tell the people they had come to do them good. They went in there and made friends with the people. These men were not in a great hurry. They waited some months and got to know a number of the workmen, and got to understand one another. They had studied the city, and the working men were astonished at how much the young fellows knew about city government, city life and education, and sanitation, cleansing and purity in all directions. One day there came a great war of labor ... In a few months these young men were the arbiters of a strike, and at a single word from them three or four thousand families were saved from being thrown out of work on a great strike. Is not that a Christian thing to do? If you understand the conception of the kingdom of God as a society of the best men working for the best ends for the improvement of human life, you will agree with me."

Sources of Illustration

Where shall we find illustrations? Sometimes, but only rarely, in books of illustrations for preachers. They do not come with freshness and telling incisiveness from that source – not often, at any rate.

Many of them may come from the Bible itself. For years my mind has toyed with the idea of producing a book of illustrations from Bible history to illustrate Bible texts. There is scope for a fine bit of literary work in that direction. The ability to touch a Bible character into life, and make it contribute to the purpose of a sermon, is much to be desired, and it may be developed. Dr. James Black's book, *An Apology for Rogues* – a book dedicated to Sunny Australia – is full of such vivid characterizations.

Here is a quotation from his sermon on Jezebel: "If we make due allowance for the natural disparity of their day and civilization, an interesting parallel may be drawn between Jezebel of Tyre and that sister queen who has been a twin enigma to historians, Mary, Queen of Scots. Both brought with them an alien outlook and culture that had no contact with the people they had to rule, and both were thrust into a somewhat passionate religious community where puritan and theological interests with which they had no sympathy were foremost ... Both were women of unbending personal will and disturbing passion, tumultuous souls, who either commanded blind adoration like Ahab's, or unsleeping distrust like Knox's. They were amazingly determined in their hearts, and as audacious and high-handed in their methods. Neither of them had any gift to understand an opponent's point of view, and they had no tact or grace in expressing their own ... Though neither could brook opposition, it was their fate to be dared and frustrated by a flaming prophet. Men in their hands were like tools, and yet men broke them. Both of them had a certain non-moral element in them that shocks us, and yet both were defeated, not so much by the religion they so openly opposed, as by moral indignation at their sins."

You may draw upon all literature for your illustrations – fiction for instance. Here is a fine illustration, which applies itself from *The Sky Pilot of No Man's Land*, by Ralph Connor. The padre is speaking, telling of the death of a corporal.

"Nothing finer in the war. There was an enemy raid coming up. The corporal had got wind of it, and called his men out. They rushed into the front line bay. Just as they got there, eight or ten of them, a live bomb fell hissing among them. They all rushed to one end of the bay, but the corporal kicked the bomb to the other end, and then threw himself on top of it. He was blown to pieces, but no one else was hurt.

During the recital of the tale, Monroe stood looking at Barry (the padre), and when he had finished his eyes were shining with tears.

'Ay, sir, he was a man, sir,' he said at length.

'Yes, you have said it, Monroe. He was a man, just a common man, but uncommonly like God, for he did the same thing. He gave himself for us.'

Monroe turned away to his work in silence."

Or poetry. There is no doubt a preacher's mind should be steeped in poetry. Poetry is picturesque, and concrete, and makes a stimulating appeal to the imagination. What a ringing character appeal there is in Edwin Markham's "Lincoln":

"He built the railpile as he built the state,
Pouring his splendid strength in every blow,
The conscience of him testing every stroke
To make his deed the measure of a man."

It is impossible for me to give even the briefest selections from various sources from which illustrations may be drawn - biography, nature, science, history, and many more.

One other source, however, must be suggested - life itself. From your own experience there will come to you, once you have developed the art, rich supplies of illustrative material. The things people say to you, and do - the chance happenings of life are full of this sort of material. You walk on to the city railway platform, and see the letters in red, "Train not going." It could go, it has the seat you would like to sit on, it is headed in the direction you want to go, but "Train not going." Could you apply that to human life? I called at the home of a friend in the apple season, and he showed me an apple tree bearing half-a-dozen kinds of lovely apples. The different varieties had been grafted into the parent stock, which was able to bear them all with equal facility. Could that be made to illustrate the rich and varied fruitfulness that is possible to the life in Christ? The world is quite full of a number of things, as R. L. Stevenson suggested; be on the watch for them and see what they have to say to your homiletical mind. Your pastoral visiting will provide you with a storehouse of material for illustrating your sermons in the most helpful way, because the experiences you have there will all concern life. Only you must be very careful that you do not reveal confidences, nor stimulate curiosity in the minds of your hearers as to whom you are speaking about. Have you noticed, when you have been listening to a sermon that was moving along steadily, what a quickening of interest there was when the preacher began to describe some personal experience? Be careful not to embellish those experiences; do not exaggerate a story to make it fit your need. If you cultivate the seeing eye you will discover an abundance of material for your needs. Be sure also that you do not make yourself the center of the experiences you relate. I remember the device of a well-known evangelist in America whose sermons were full of personal experience – he always made them personal, even if the only relation he himself had to one was that it happened to the niece of a woman whom his wife once met on a railway station. You do not have to impose yourself to make your experience either interesting or effective.

Your Task

It is imperative then, if you wish to be a really good preacher, that you learn the art of illustration. Many hearers will not get your ideas unless you put them in concrete form. Not that you should make your sermon a string of anecdotes – you must not pack your sermon with illustrations. And please do not use simpering sentimental stories, nor too many of the tearful kind, if any at all. The work must be simply, finely, chastely done. You may not have the gift. Dr. James Black, one of the greatest preachers in Scotland for a generation, whose visit to Australia some of us remember with gratitude, said that his early sermons were as devoid of illustrations as a bald man of hair. He is a master of the art now, and his skill in it is one of the secrets of his success.

My fear is that you may acknowledge the truth of what I say, and fail to make the effort to master the technique of discovering, creating and using illustrations in your sermons. It is not a subject merely to read about in an interested sort of way, but one to attack with enthusiastic courage that we may conquer it and make it our own. Work! That is the secret of success. *"How did Dr. Fosdick become the great preacher he is?"* asks Edgar De Witt Jones, himself a great preacher, and answers: *"By the hardest kind of work, unceasing laborious toil, painstaking industry."* He spends his mornings where no messages can get him, no telephone reach him, and no visitors are admitted. In such seclusion he "toils terribly" over his sermons. We may never be preachers of the dimensions of Dr. Fosdick, but we may be like him in some respects. We may, by diligence and hard work, become "up-to-capacity" preachers, one hundred per cent efficient in the use of the talents we possess to develop and use.

Eye and Ear

It is a common and edifying custom, when addressing children's assemblies, to use models, pictures, or some form of illustrative material which appeals to the eye. The same method may sometimes be used with advantage in ordinary sermon work. Recently in a sermon in which I was discussing immeasurable factors in personality and life, I drew from my pocket a three-feet rule and measured my Bible – nine inches by five. I picked up another book – much larger in bulk – eleven inches by eight. The latter was an old college annual, of interest to a very limited number of people when it was published, and of rapidly decreasing interest with every year that passed, while the Bible is a book that has shaped the centuries, is published in a thousand tongues, and grows in power forever. There was no question about the quickened interest in the few moments that the illustration occupied. No doubt this is a method that should be used with restraint. Any kind of dramatic presentation that can be given to a sermon is of interest value.

Once or twice I have put my sermon into dialogue form, in which two people were represented in discussion of some living subject. It was well worthwhile, but it is a method that needs to be used with great care, for you must not seem to give one side—your side—a crushing advantage in the discussion, for it never happens that way when two strong, well informed men discuss worth-while subjects. Another method is to select a capable opponent (for the purpose of discussion), to work over the subject together thoroughly, and to present the material to the congregation in the form of a discussion.

For Review:

1. Find an illustration in the form of a story to illustrate the text *"One's life does not consist in the abundance of the things he possesses"* (Luke 12:15).

2. Illustrate in some way the statement while we do not look at the things which are seen, but at the things which are not seen. *"For the things which are seen* ARE *temporary, but the things which are not seen are eternal"* (2 Corinthians 4:18).

13. A Word Fitly Spoken

"Oh! the power of words! With them we sway men's minds at will. Let me call your attention to the sea. The Sea! Close your eyes and look at it as you saw it last summer. Think of its waves away, away out yonder. See that ripple of white running along on the crest of the nearer one – see it now as it sheens and advances in wreaths of delicate foam almost to your feet and then rolls playfully back in beautiful sheets to be lost in the next incoming tide. See the old mast out there and the sails that dot the horizon. You see them all now! Why? Words only words!" Thus Dr. Conwell drew upon the imagination and described the power of words.

The writer of Proverbs, in a beautiful and suggestive simile, said *"A word fitly spoken IS LIKE apples of gold In settings of silver"* (Proverbs 25:11).

As a preacher you use words for the conveyance of your thought. Not all words are fitly spoken, unfortunately. Long ago there were men who darkened counsel by words without knowledge (Job 38:2). Astute men have often used words to conceal thought. It has been said that words are like glass – they obscure what they do not help us to see. If we have really been called of God to the work of preaching, a divine obligation rests upon us to see that "words of grace" characterize our public ministry of the Word.

Learn Words

A man who depends upon words to imbibe knowledge and express his thoughts must necessarily become acquainted with words. The ordinary man feels no need to learn words – a limited number comes to his use in his daily experience, and he is able to get along very well. It is different with the preacher. He must read books. If he is to do his duty adequately he must be able to read worthwhile books. He is called upon to address all types of men – scholarly men and illiterate men. He must know words.

How do men learn words? I know of no alternative to steady plodding work. There is great value, of course, in wide reading. That in itself is bound to be a valuable method of learning the meaning and use of words. It can hardly take the place of the steady use of the dictionary. My own method for years was to use pencil and notebook, and write the words of which I did not know either the meaning or the pronunciation, and the dictionary was in constant use. Long before I left the farm I was accustomed to take lists of words and their meanings out into the fields, and memorize them as I followed the plough. The words I learnt when, as a boy of sixteen, I waded through Farrar's *Life and Work of St. Paul*! Please do not examine me to see if I remember them all. I learned them all, and it was no small task. In those youthful days, in the little country church where we had no minister, I preached with some regularity, and I liked to use the words I had learned. I quite well remember a day when I was preaching on the inspiration of the apostles, and concluded the sermon by saying they *"spoke as the amanuenses of God."* I remember also the comments that followed, which led me to avoid the use of large words altogether – a practice which I have tried to follow to this very day. I did not, however, abandon the study of words. For many years those interminable lists were my constant friends, and provided one of the most valuable disciplines of my life. Give yourselves to this painstaking drill if you wish to become effective preachers. Pick up words as you would pick up valuable shells on the seashore.

The Use of Words

Learn to use words. One may acquire the knowledge of many words without knowing how to use them well. A preacher needs not only to read books of doctrine and theology and philosophy to inform his mind. He should read some books to learn how to use words. There are many books of this nature. Shakespeare is always recommended for this purpose. Fortunately the one book the preacher is supposed to make his constant friend is one that all masters of English prose recommend without fail – the Bible.

Someone has said that whatever might be true of the first writers of the books of the Bible, the English translators of the Bible were certainly inspired, so simple and true were they in their use of words.

Authorities always emphasize the strength and beauty of the Anglo-Saxon words, as compared with those of Latin and Greek origin. We may not all be well versed enough in the ancient languages to know which is which. It is sufficient for practical purposes to remember that as a rule the short crisp words are the strong words. A schoolmaster (so it is said) saw a farmer working with a spade on the roadside. He said, "Are you excavating a subterranean channel?" The farmer said "No, I'm digging a ditch." Meiklejohn, in his *The Art of Writing English* (a most valuable book, by the way) tells of an alderman in the city of London who was offended when one of his colleagues proposed to inscribe on the tombstone of the great statesman George Channing, the simple words, "He died poor." He thought it would be much more appropriate to say, "He expired in circumstances of extreme indigence." Educated people do not write or speak like that now. Let me impress the lesson by saying, Avoid grandiose verbosity! Following is a remarkable example of the vigor and force that may be secured by the use of words of only one syllable:

Think not that strength lies in the big round word,
Or that the brief and plain must needs be weak.
To whom can this be true who once has heard
The cry for help, the tongue that all men speak,
When want, or woe, or fear is in the throat,
So that each word gasped out is like a shriek
Pressed from the sore heart or a strange wild note
Sung by some fay or fiend? There is a strength
Which dies if stretched too far or spun too fine;
Which has more height than breadth, more depth than length.

Let but this force of thought and speech be mine,
And he that will may take the sleek, fat phrase,
Which glows and burns not, though it gleam and shine--
Light, but not heat-a flash, but not a blaze!
Nor is it mere strength that the short word boasts;
It serves of more than fight or storm to tell--
The roar of waves that clash on rock-bound coasts,
The crash of tall trees when the wild winds swell,
The roar of guns, the groans of men that die
On blood-stained fields. It has a voice as well
For them that far off on their sick-beds lie,
For them that weep, for them that mourn the dead;
For them that laugh, and dance, and clap the hand,
To Joy's quick step, as well as Grief's slow tread.

The sweet, plain words we learned at first keep time,
And though the theme be sad, or gay, or grand,
With each, with all, these may be made to chime,
In thought, or speech, or song, or prose, or rhyme.
--J. ADDISON ALEXANDER.

Short Sentences

Use not only simple rugged words, but short clear-cut sentences as well. Do not talk in the following manner unless you are trying to induce sleep in your congregation:

In addressing sinners, then, in a careless, unawakened state, I am not prepared to say that the subject here treated on would be of any immediate, practical use: but as it forms one important branch of sacred truth, and frequently occurs in the general tenor of apostolic teaching; moreover, as every spiritual requisition involves the necessity of this divine agency, it surely ought to occupy a conspicuous place in our general exhibitions of the economy of divine grace.

Apart from anything else, you can never hold attention in that way. Break the sentence up into four, and it will become much more intelligible, even though it is heavy with long words.

Use of Synonyms

One of the most rewarding studies in the use of words is that of synonyms, that is, of words that are similar in meaning. The appreciation of delicate differences in the meaning of words may well be a coveted accomplishment. A book that has been on my library shelves during all my public life is *Roget's Thesaurus of English Words and Phrases*. The book is nearly one hundred years old, and has been published so often that the original plates were worn out. It is still a standard work, and one of the best of its kind. I could not begin to tell the value this book has been to me. Its use is especially to help in the study of words and their synonyms and their opposites. It will be found a profitable exercise to make lists of words in common use, and write down any synonyms you remember.

Take, for instance, the verb "claim." What synonyms can you recall? "Maintain, aver, affirm, assert." When you come to the end of your own resources, Roget will probably supply some more - "contend, say, state, certify." The finer shades of meaning can only be fully appreciated by one who reads extensively among the best masters of English literature. We often see in the humor columns of our papers the alleged attempts of foreigners to use our words, and they can be very amusing. In our work as preachers the use of words in incorrect relations may or may not be amusing, it will rather be an occasion for sadness and annoyance to those who enjoy the refinements of language.

It is not possible here to make an extensive discussion of the use of words. My purpose is to emphasize the importance of such a study, and to indicate how much is missed if one is ignorant of the power of words. A preacher's resources should include a wide vocabulary, not, as someone has said, "*that you may use many or large words, but that you may use few, and those few fit for the occasion.*" Only ignorant people could be impressed by a flow of large words from a preacher's lips, and only an ignorant preacher would use such words in presenting the message of the gospel. It may be necessary for a lawyer to be voluminous and involved in his deed of transfer or whatever it is he writes - he has the gift of making his work seem worth the fee that it costs. It may be necessary for the scientist to use words of Latin and Greek derivation to express his meaning in exact definition, but a preacher's business is to speak clearly.

Speak Clearly

Herbert Spencer once wrote a famous definition of evolution. "*It is,*" he said, "*the integration of matter and concomitant dissipation of motion, from an indefinite incoherent homogeneity to a definite heterogeneity, with structure and function, during which the retained motion undergoes a parallel transformation."*

While we may perhaps thank Spencer for his illuminating statement, we shall not, I trust, imitate his style.

Clearness in speaking, to be sure, is not merely a matter of words. To speak clearly one must think clearly. A preacher needs to think through his subject matter thoroughly before he attempts to preach it. Our earlier chapters have described the art of building the outline of a sermon, but always there has been the steady emphasis on the need of amplifying, clarifying and enriching the material to be presented. There are some subjects that cannot be made very clear to the ordinary man – questions of metaphysics, for example, but they should be avoided in our preaching. Some Biblical subjects which lie at the very heart of Christian doctrine, such as The Atonement, or Election, will never be easy to deal with either, and we shall do well to discuss only such aspects of great themes as have become clear to our own minds.

Words have somewhat of personality, it seems to me. Ruskin suggests something like this when he says an educated gentleman *"is learned in the peerage of words; knows the words of true descent and ancient blood, at a glance, from words of modern canaille."* I doubt if I mean just the same thing, however. Ruskin moved among the aristocracy of words in a very beautiful way, but to me, whether it is of noble descent or not, "a word's a word for a' that.' (Though that statement is printed within quotation marks it is not a quotation really.) I am thinking now of the quality of words as they come to our ears. There are rich words, and poor; strong words, and weak. The way we put words together in sentences also will contribute largely to our style of speech.

Vigorous Utterance

Some speakers are simply tame. Some are tame even when they are not lacking in physical energy and vociferous utterance. Matthew Arnold once criticized the English style of General Grant. Grant was one of Mark Twain's heroes, and the celebrated humorist came to the defense. He said in part: *"There is that about the sun which makes us forget his spots, and when we think of General Grant our pulses quicken and his grammar vanishes; we only remember that this is the simple soldier who, all untaught of the silken-phrase makers, linked words together with an art surpassing the art of schools and put into them a something which will still bring to American ears the roll of his vanished drums and the tread of his marching hosts ... Think of those thunderous phrases: 'unconditional and immediate surrender.' 'I propose to move immediately upon your works,' 'I propose to fight it out on this line if it takes all summer.'* Mr. Arnold would doubtless claim that this last phrase is not strictly grammatical, yet it did certainly wake up this nation as a hundred million tons of a No. 1, fool-proof, hard-boiled, hide-bound grammar from another mouth could not have done." I have selected this passage, not alone for the samples of strong simple speech that Mark Twain quotes, but for the vigor of his own language in describing it. Be on the watch for strong words in powerful sentences. Look for good phrases too – *"Study phrases,"* said Robert Blatchford, *"seek them, hoard them, prize them; keep them bright. Collect and treasure phrases as you would collect and treasure the rarest pieces of old blue china."*

The Preacher an Artist

The image making faculty is one of the most interesting and useful that a preacher possesses. To call to mind vivid and varied pictures, and to develop the ability to describe them, is a powerful element in good speaking. This art, like all the arts, can be developed. When in your reading you come to a word picture – a description that makes you see – pause awhile to study how it is done.

It is evening. The sun is near to setting. The air is still and the sea is calm. As the sun sinks towards the bright clouds they assume fantastic shapes. A column of burnished brass runs from our feet to the western horizon, where land and sea and cloud merge into a haze of bright yellow and saffron. Over there a point of land jutting out towards the gleaming shaft of light is swathed in opalescent glow. As the sun sinks out of sight, the moon, almost at the full appears over Mt. Dandenong, and soon another column, a shimmering silvery sheen, stretches away over the waters to the east. Purple clouds to the north still catch the light of the departing sun, and reflect it in rose-pink tints on the glazed surface of the water.

That is a picture as real, though of a different sort, as the pictures you see in the City Library. You see the setting sun and the rising moon and the varied lights on sea and cloud. Try your own skill at such picturing. Look steadily at a storm, a bush fire, or the sky at night, and paint the picture you see in words. Such developed skill will vastly help you in preaching.

There is another way in which the artistry of words may be and ought to be practiced, and that is by the use of the various figures of speech which adorn our language. The teaching of our Lord was richly adorned with similes and allegories and other forms which revealed his image-making power. Bond, in *Homiletics of Jesus*, says that at least sixty-two figures of speech are used in the Sermon on the Mount.

To illustrate the remarkable way in which such pictures may adorn our speech, I shall quote a few lines from Patrick Henry's famous oration – *"Give me Liberty or Give me Death."*

"Mr. President, it is natural to man to indulge in (1) the illusions of hope. We are apt (2) to shut our eyes against a painful truth, and (3) listen to the song of the siren, till she transforms us into beasts. (4) Is this the part of wise men, engaged in a great and arduous struggle for liberty? (5) Are we disposed to he of the number of those who, (6) having eyes see not, and having cars hear not, the things which so nearly concern their temporal salvation? ... (7) I have but one lamp by which my feet are guided, and that is (8) the lamp of experience."

Note the various figures which are in this brief quotation. I have numbered the most obvious of them. (1) is a metaphor; (2) another metaphor; (3) an allusion to Grecian mythology; (4) a rhetorical interrogation; (5) another rhetorical interrogation; (6) a scriptural allusion; (7) another scriptural allusion; (8) a metaphor.

Such imagery not only enriches language; it tends to give the speaker interest and power. All good preachers are proficient in it. I open a volume of *Maclaren's Expositions* at random, and the very first line has this metaphor: "*There will come a film over Hope's blue eye.*" On the opposite page is another: "*The Church is God's trumpet.*" I glance at H. Emerson Fosdick and find a striking simile about "*lives isolated like bottles in the rain.*" I take from my shelves a volume of sermons by A. J. Gossip, and on the page at which it opens is this: "*How often in our history a door has opened in a dead blank wall, where certainly there was no door.*" The speech of all great preachers is filled with such arresting figures of speech. We may use them too. Indeed we must, for such imagery is the chief thing which gives interest and beauty to abstract truths and dry facts, and rescues our speech from the deep river of dull monotony.

Here we must stop. In many other ways we might have illustrated the power of "*a word fitly spoken,*" but at least enough has been said to open this vast field of opportunity to study and research, enough, I trust, to awaken a divine discontent in the heart of every reader who has not in some degree mastered these accomplishments, and to stimulate him to give sincere and constant attention to their attainment.

For Review:

1. Exercise your mind in discovering synonyms for the following words: Search, Fashioned, Integrity.

2. Find similes for justice, truth, mercy.

3. Invent metaphors for reason, nature, knowledge.

4. Make sentences in which the following phrases are introduced: The eloquence of God; the wounds of self-love; the gnawing of envy.

5. Write a picture in words of (1) a storm, (2) a football scrimmage, (3) the sky at night.

14. The Sermon in Action

The moment of crisis comes when you stand before your congregation to preach the message – the best which your hours of toil and the resources of your knowledge and imagination have been able to produce. Everything depends upon what you do with your sermon in the next twenty or twenty-five minutes in which you seek to give it expression. And that depends upon another set of factors altogether: your bearing, your manner, the management of your breath, the control of your voice, the enunciation of your words. You are now in need of another course of training, to enable you to capitalize the results of your week's labor. A man with goods to sell needs the gift of salesmanship; a man with capital to use requires the business ability to invest it. A preacher with a message to deliver must have the necessary gifts to present it to his people. The sermon which is the result of patient study and homiletical skill is of no value at all to his congregation unless he preaches it; it may be worse than useless if he preaches it badly.

It would be fitting therefore if we now set out on another course of studies to learn how to make the message effective on the day of unburdening. The fact that the study of the art of sermon construction has occupied thirteen chapters, and the study of the sermon in action is to be dealt with in one, is no indication of their relative importance. The delivery of the sermon is of primary importance, and one of the reasons why preaching has fallen upon evil days is that so many preachers are content to mooch along in their pulpit work without any effort to develop the latent resources they possess. It involves a course of studies in itself – a course which every man who dares to stand up to speak the oracles of God, should undertake with resolution and unquenchable persistence, and the purpose of this closing chapter is to unveil both the need and the possibilities of this aspect of preaching work.

Stance

Let us begin with stance. That is a sporting term, I know, but I do not recall any other quite so good for the idea I have in mind. It is the position of the player's feet in relation to each other and to the ball when he is making a stroke.

That's it exactly. The position of a preacher's feet relative to one another and his audience is a matter of consequence. Recall some attitudes you have seen. Here is a man standing flatfooted, heels together and toes out at an angle of ninety degrees – an uninspiring attitude. Here is another with a foot sticking out eighteen inches from the other, poised on its heel, with the toes pointed to heaven. A preacher should take care that he does not appear gawky. Fortunately, or otherwise, for some men, the pulpit or the desk hides a multitude of faults. A student whom I criticized last week for bending at the knees – a very ugly gesture – when he wished to emphasize a point, remarked that the desk would hide it when he was preaching. It is a pity when any man will try to shelter himself behind some object to hide faults of which he should rid himself. There will come days when a preacher stands on an open platform for special addresses. If, sheltering behind a pulpit he has developed unfortunate habits of bearing he feels clumsy, awkward, and probably looks worse than he feels. Even so simple a habit as holding on to the pulpit proves to be a terribly disturbing one if a pulpit is not there. My friend Gilbert E. Chandler believed that he had a body every part of which should be made effective for preaching. *"An actor doesn't hide his legs behind a desk,"* he once said to me; *"he learns how to conduct himself before his audience."* The best position for the feet is to have one slightly in advance of the other, with the heel of one about three inches from the instep of the other, and the toes at an angle of forty or forty-five degrees. The weight normally should be on the rear foot, though it may be transferred to the other, or borne by both feet, according to the nature of the utterance. There should, of course, be perfect freedom for any movement that may be required. One must not be so stiff in his stand that he looks as if a foot movement would be tantamount to breaking one of the Ten Commandments. On the other hand, movement should not be excessive. Some preachers roam about the platform like a caged lion, but in doing so they are not nearly so impressive as the king of beasts.

Expanded Chest

Stand erect! The best way to do this is to maintain an expanded chest. If a speaker does this he not only ensures an erect attitude; he also by the same token fulfills all the various instructions to be found in text books about keeping the lungs properly filled for public speech. This expansion of the chest may be made by muscular effort, quite apart from the inflation of the lungs. To know what is meant, stand with your back to a wall, touching the wall with head and body. Then while holding the body exactly in the attitude thus assumed, move from the wall slightly, and you will realize that you are "carrying your chest." Learn to carry it in this way – maintain an expanded chest – whenever you are standing or walking, until it becomes your habitual attitude. It will do a number of things for you, all of them good. It will prevent you from becoming round shouldered, as many young students are prone to do. It will give you easy control of breath in preaching. It will prevent you from degenerating into that most pathetic sight, often to be seen in preachers of middle age, of a man standing to deliver a message with ribs collapsed and stomach protruding. Pray to be saved from that, and answer your prayer by learning to maintain always the expanded chest. Alexander Watson, the world-renowned public speaker, who about twenty years ago delighted Australian audiences night after night through a long season with his public recitals, said that this position of the expanded chest is one that all skilled public speakers assume, consciously or unconsciously, at the beginning of a speech.

There should be no exaggeration, nothing of a "sergeant-major attitude," involving strained rigidity. The position may require effort at first to maintain it on and off the platform but it becomes natural after a while, is a tonic to health, and a source of confidence to the preacher. Some men will not need to concern themselves about this. Alexander Watson, in his book, *Speak Out*, tells who they are. You may wish to know if you are exempt. They are "*Phlegmatic, unemotional speakers ... and those who speak with a maximum of head and a minimum of heart, especially if they never have occasion to address very large audiences.*"

Gestures

Gestures may be effective aids to public speech. They may be a real hindrance. The art of gesturing needs cultivation; please note I did not say artificiality. There is a world of difference between art and artificiality. One is from above, the other from beneath. There is nothing more offensive than artificiality in gesture. One can put up with it from "trained" elocutionists at a social gathering if a good supper is to follow, but you cannot endure it in a preacher. Gestures, however, are usually not so artificial as meaningless, uncoordinated movements that express nothing, and are merely the release of pent-up energy. Avoid clenching the fist – I saw a preacher say "*God is love,*" and he shook a clenched fist at his congregation all the while, the tense attitude not only making him ridiculous, but giving a strident note to his voice quite unbecoming to the sentiment he was expressing. Keep your hands out of your pockets.

I have not yet quite recovered from the shock I received last year when a senior student – almost a finished product of the college – stood with both hands in his pockets reading to his people a great message from the Word of God. Let your hands hang easily by your side, the fingers touching lightly on the trousers. They must hang easily. If they are held stiffly, they will seem awkward. The most natural and graceful position for the hands is by the side, even if it feels uncomfortable, as I can testify it does till you become accustomed to it. They may be held in front, for a change, or at the back. If you put them behind you, see that they do not drag the shoulders down, and collapse the ribs – place them behind the waist, and keep your chest expanded. In your gestures, never move your hands from the wrists or elbows alone there should always be movement from the shoulders. A preacher who makes practically all his gestures outward from the elbows, in the middle zone, merely giving a senseless flip of the hand in the same way, whether he is describing a burial or announcing the trumpet blast of Gabriel at the resurrection, is merely an annoyance. Learn to raise your hands high when you are expressing elevated thoughts. Stand before a mirror and study your movements. Women have no compunctions about using a mirror, and quite commonly they achieve good results, according to their tastes, of course. You may not be worth looking at in a mirror for general purposes, but it becomes an essential thing to a man who really wants to make the best of his gestures in preaching. It was a man, not a woman, according to James, who looked at himself in a mirror and straightway went away and forgot what he looked like. Modern psychology teaches us that we easily forget what is unpleasant. Only you must not forget when you are studying gesture work. Look and look again, experimenting with the way you move your hands and arms, until you can do it with some measure of grace. Study other preachers and learn from their gestures, good and bad – especially the latter, for the field of study is so much more extensive. Ask some discerning friend who has good judgment, to watch you, and to give you the benefit of his observations. Study some good treatise on gesture; it will teach you the sort of thing to attempt. Always maintain a healthy fear of artificiality, use – I repeat it, sir – use the mirror, and always pray

> "Oh, would some power the gift give us
> To see ourselves as others see us!"

Voice Control

The voice is the preacher's chief means of conveying his message to his hearers, yet it is probably correct to say that comparatively few men give any real attention to the cultivation of a good voice. A few fortunate people do not need to; without effort they have dropped into a natural easy way of using their voices with brilliance and power. It ought to be so with all living things. It is with most of them. The magpie reaches perfection in his rich full tones which delight us so much in the freshness of the spring morning. I have wondered at the absolute control a dog has of all the apparatus of voice production – I have often studied him, especially at night when he would not let me sleep. It is different with humans, for the most part. Perhaps because of restraints thrown about us in youth, perhaps because of a growing sense of our inability ever to reach the heights of attainment to which our souls aspire, most of us do not use our voices well. The astounding thing is that most preachers do not care that this is so. In my city there are many men, members of Rostrum Clubs, who meet every week to improve the quality of their public speaking. Preachers, because of their divine calling, should be, of all men, the most ambitious to cultivate the power of their voices to the glory of God. A preacher once wrote me – he is in heaven now, and would not mind if I quoted him – "*My old voice is constantly turning me down. I think of training, but feel the time is too precious to be spent in voice training. However, I have spoiled a number of my best prepared addresses with gulping and 'fizzling out'.*" But for the old motto, *De Mortuis nil nisi bonum.*

I hardly know what I wouldn't say. "Best prepared addresses! "Spoiled!" "Fizzling out!" "Time too precious to be spent in voice training!" Probably his words tell their own story sufficiently well.

Having confessed someone else's sins, perhaps I had better confess my own. When I was young I had some good instruction in voice training, but did not use it. After four years of preaching in Australia I went to America and spent four years there. No voice training – "*time was too precious to be spent in voice training.*" I came back to Australia then, with the stamp of the university and of American experience on me. Something was expected of me, naturally. But before long my throat gave way through wrong use, and many of my best sermons were spoiled "*with gulping and fizzling out.*" I had loved singing, solos and part singing, but I could sing no more. Two doctors told me they could do nothing for me – it was "*clergymen's sore throat,*" and I should have to get on as best I could. Fortunately there then came into my hands a little book, *How to Train the Speaking Voice*, by Thomas Tait, M.A., B.D. It taught me that my trouble was constriction of the throat, and it gave one simple exercise for overcoming it. I set to work diligently, and in three weeks I was able again to take my place in part-singing, and from that day to this I have had no difficulty with my throat.

Even though a preacher may have experienced no collapse of that sort, it does not follow that he is using his voice effectively. The human voice is such a wonderful instrument that it will well repay a preacher to seek to develop pure quality, and resonance, and modulation. How thin and flat and toneless some voices are! Like most musical instruments, the human speaking apparatus has a motor, a vibrator, and a resonator. The motor is the lungs, the vibrator is the vocal chords, and the resonator is the nasal and mouth cavities. The lungs, in speaking, are (or should be) controlled by the muscles at the base of the chest. These abdominal muscles steady the expenditure of breath in ordinary speaking, and provide the power of explosive utterance when it is required. One can always tell whether explosive commands like *"Charge, Chester, charge! On, Stanley, on!"* are delivered by the vigorous action of the abdominal muscles, as they ought to be, or by a strain on the vocal chords. In the latter case the effect is always flat and poor. The quality of resonance, again, adds greatly to the beauty of the speaking voice, and it is possible for all to acquire it in some degree. Neglect not the gift that is in thee!

Enunciation

Probably one of the most distressing features of faulty speaking is lack of proper enunciation. A group of young college students, who aspire to be ministers of the Word, who have done a little public speaking in Christian Endeavor and similar meetings, may be presumed to be as effective in enunciation as most people who have not had special training, but it is remarkable how much training they need, as a rule, in this direction. This fact is mentioned in order that other men, who do not come to college, but who seek to prepare themselves for the work of local preaching, or to equip themselves for other kinds of work, may feel the need of practice in articulate utterance.

And what shall I more say? For time would fail me to tell of emphasis, and inflection, and pitch, and rate, and force, and pausing, all of them worthy of earnest study and diligent practice. The sincere worker may well be appalled by the magnitude of the task of mastering even in an elementary way the art of public speaking, until he cries, Who is sufficient for these things? And provided he has something of the grit and willingness to work that the apostle Paul had, he may, like him, hear the voice of the Lord saying, My grace is sufficient for thee.

15. Simple Exercises in Voice Development

A few simple exercises, diligently and constantly practiced, will do much to help in developing the quality of the voice, and in avoiding the most common faults in speech.

1. To avoid throat strain. The voice must be trained to come from the hard palate, near the front upper teeth, and not from the soft palate, back near the throat. Some sounds naturally come off the hard palate, OO for instance. Other sounds are not easily kept out of the throat, AH particularly. You cannot constrict the throat when you say OO, but you can very easily when you say AH. Try them. You can, if you try, hurt your throat in saying words like Heart, Guard, Father. It is almost impossible to do so in uttering Booth, Root, Two. The problem is to learn to sound all vowels off the hard palate.

For an exercise, sound OO-OH-AH. Shape the lips into a small round aperture for OO, a little larger but still round for OH, and open the mouth for AH. But that AH must be made to come from the hard palate, as does OO. Practice a number of times, on different pitches, and listen carefully every time that AH never becomes throaty. It is worse than useless if not done correctly.

Another exercise for the same purpose is the constant use of the word LET. You cannot pronounce it except on the hard palate, where all sounds should be produced. Sing LET at different pitches, with upward and downward inflection, and with different degrees of force. Then repeat some words, listening carefully to note that they are correctly placed on the hard palate.

Here is the exercise:

LET LET LET LET LET LET LE-E-E-T, etc.

"Tell me not in mournful numbers Life is but an empty dream."

LET LET, etc.

2. To develop resonance. Hum and pronounce the sound MAW. Hold the lips lightly, but completely closed for a prolonged hum, and open out on the word. Force the breath into the air passages of the head and face during the humming. Practice sentences like "The thUNDer RUMbled aMONG the HILLS," aiming for resonance on the N, and M sounds.

3. To develop the abdominal muscles. One must be able to do this if he is to speak with power and effective modulation.

Note that the waist muscles are used in all natural exercises involving violent expulsion of breath, as in coughing, laughing, and yawning. The same muscles are required for powerful speaking.

(a) Contract and expand the waist muscles by muscular effort, apart from using the breath.

(b) Contract the waist muscles as you say HA, HA, HA; HUR-RAH.

(c) Shout HELP, expelling the sound with a violent action of the waist muscles.

Persistent long continued practice will be necessary if this action of the abdominal muscles has not previously been developed. The muscular action, without sound, can be practiced anywhere, while standing, walking, etc. The co-ordination of the muscular movement with the utterances of the syllables must be mastered. Practice the following sentence, using the violent contraction of the muscles on the accented syllables:

"ARM! ARM! it IS, it IS the CANnon's OPening ROAR."

4. For Purity of tone.

Pronounce E, A, AW, AH, OH, OO.

Pronounce same with rising and falling inflexion.

Sing LE, LA, LAW, LAH, LOH, LOO.

The abdominal muscles should be used lightly on these exercises.

5. For enunciation. Read passages in syllables, as: When pub-lic bod-ies are to be ad-dressed on mo-men-tous o-cca-sions, when great in-ter-ests are at stake and strong pa-ssions ex-cit-ed, noth-ing is val-u-a-ble in speech, fur-ther than as it is con-nect-ed with high in-tell-ec-tu-al and mor-al en-dow-ments.

Do not run any of these syllables together in any way. After reading it aloud thus two or three times, read it naturally.

A short regular exercise each day (choose your own selections) will greatly increase your consciousness of syllables, and improve your general enunciation. You will not then say "Through this the well-beloved Brutus tabbed" when it should be "Brutus stabbed"; nor will you say "His beer descending" when you should say "His beard descending."

6. Always allow the lower jaw to work freely. Open the mouth well on each syllable in the following: "Say there! What do you say? Pale ale fails to regale."

Voice culture is as essential to good speaking as it is to good singing. "Study to show thyself approved unto God, a workman that needeth not to be ashamed."

THANK YOU FOR
INVESTING IN THIS BOOK!

If you'd like to see some of our many resources for Bible Study leaders and Pastors, please go to:
http://www.pastorshelper.com

I hope to hear from you soon! May God bless you as you continue to serve Him.

In Christ,

Barry L. Davis

CPSIA information can be obtained at www.ICGtesting.com
Printed in the USA
BVOW06s0148191215

430638BV00014B/368/P